PRICE
Catalysts

PRICE Catalysts

Proven Strategies for Spotting Profitable Stock Investments

Jim Osman

Harriman House

HARRIMAN HOUSE LTD
3 Viceroy Court
Bedford Road
Petersfield
Hampshire
GU32 3LJ
GREAT BRITAIN
Tel: +44 (0)1730 233870

Email: enquiries@harriman-house.com
Website: harriman.house

First published in 2025.

Hardback ISBN: 978-0-85719-855-6
Paperback ISBN: 978-1-80409-097-8
eBook ISBN: 978-0-85719-856-3

British Library Cataloguing in Publication Data
A CIP catalogue record for this book can be obtained from the British Library.

Printed and bound in India by Repro India Ltd

For sale in the Indian subcontinent only

Contents

Introduction: If You Need a Friend, Get a Dog

THOUGH THE WORLD of money can sometimes seem complicated and unreachable, when I consider what inspired my enthusiasm for catalyst investing, it all comes back to the 1987 movie *Wall Street*. I related especially to the excitement, the stakes, and the realization that behind every deal is strategy and tenacity. These "special situations," however, are far more than the rush of a sale. They are about revealing latent value in locations most people ignore.

When I consider the development of corporate raiders in the 1980s and 1990s – people like Carl Icahn and Michael Milken – I see how these important players changed the market via mergers and leveraged buyouts. Their audacious actions established whole sectors and opened the path for what we today refer to as unique events. This is about the inventiveness needed to unleash shareholder value in original ways, not about avarice or gloss. These techniques originally piqued my curiosity and helped me to develop a career based on locating those understated treasures.

Special situations thrill me; what I want to communicate in this book is how these possibilities offer an edge – through spin-offs, restructuring, or sophisticated financial plays. From a driven child in

South London to starting The Edge, a spin-off research firm, my path has been one of continual hunt for these undervalued events.

Every chapter in this book is meant to guide you further into this area so you understand how to seize possibilities most missed by other investors. Whether you are a novice player or a seasoned expert, I am sure you will find something worthwhile here.

Catalyst investing: why waiting for the right moment outperforms traditional value strategies

I am a non-traditional investor.

What does that mean exactly?

It means that overall, you can't tell me something is cheap purely on its numbers. I look for catalysts to move price to value, because as we know, cheap can stay cheap and even get cheaper.

According to conventional value investing, we should purchase underpriced assets and only wait for them to grow gradually. But suppose waiting isn't sufficient? Value investing can produce profits, but it usually fails without a catalyst – an event or element that causes the market to reconsider the actual worth of an asset.

This is where catalyst investment comes in.

Catalyst investors deliberately search for events or moments – such as mergers, spin-offs, or earnings surprises – that can spark a stock's revaluation instead of merely hoarding cheap equities and hoping the market catches up. Usually resulting in faster and more notable profits than conventional value methods alone, these catalysts act as a signal for the market to acknowledge latent value.

What is catalyst investing?

Purchasing cheap stocks with the hope that a particular event will release their actual worth is the essence of catalyst investing. Catalyst investment depends on market-moving events that act as triggers for revaluation, unlike conventional value investing, which concentrates on basic criteria such as price-to-earnings ratios or book value. These events – mergers, spin-offs, income shocks, legislative changes, or management changes – act as the spark that drives the market to acknowledge the underlying value of an asset.

The main distinctions are in market impression and timing. Catalyst investors concentrate on the circumstances that can lead to this realization, whereas classic value investors patiently wait for the market to catch up with the intrinsic worth of a firm. Catalysts turn inactive assets into active performers, giving what may otherwise be slow investments momentum. Targeting and waiting for these events will help catalyst investors release a lot of upside potential more quickly than those depending just on value principles. In the end, catalyst investing adds a strategic dimension that lets investors take advantage of revaluation prospects when the market would have otherwise passed over them.

The pitfall of traditional value investing

Sometimes traditional value investing fails since merely pointing out an underpriced item does not ensure the market will value an asset as it deserves. For years some equities remain "cheap" without any notable movement, leaving investors hoping for appreciation that never materializes. This is sometimes referred to as a value trap, in which case low values entice investors but overlook the essential component of a trigger to release the potential of the asset.

Many times, investors purchase stocks just based on low price-to-earnings ratios or book value, believing the market will reprice the asset finally. These equities sometimes underperform, nevertheless, without a catalyst to spur revaluation. One classic example is Sears, which sank as the market saw no bright future for the business even if it was appreciated aesthetically for years. Sears kept spiralling down without a clear catalyst – such as a successful reorganization or a turnaround in company operations – and it failed to reward patient investors.

Why catalyst investing outperforms

Catalyst investing provides a strong means to bring undervalued assets to life, therefore inducing market revaluation and releasing latent value. Catalyst investing avoids value traps by concentrating on events that compel a re-evaluation, while conventional value techniques may leave investors waiting forever for the market to appreciate the value of an asset.

Catalyst investing offers an advantage that can greatly exceed more traditional methods for investors ready to do the study and practice patience. Investors may set themselves to profit from times of market transition by spotting important catalysts and knowing the larger forces acting in the market. Although timing and strategy are crucial, for those who grasp this method the benefits usually outweigh those of conventional value investing alone.

PART ONE

THEORY OF SPECIAL SITUATIONS

CHAPTER 1

The Secrets to Winning at the Stock Market Roulette Wheel

- Investing or Gambling?
- What Do Investors Fear the Most?
- Always Start with Evaluating Risk
- How The Structure of Your Investment Should Look
- Final Areas to Consider

Investing or Gambling?

When it comes to the stock market, are you an investor or a gambler? Most would want to be labeled an investor, of course. Nobody calls themselves a gambler. The word gives rise to ideas of addiction and recklessness. Those with gambling disorder are looked upon as "greedy" and "irresponsible". They are thought to be at fault for their difficulties, even to the point that others may avoid interacting with them.

But hold on a second. At their core, investing and gambling both involve the use of capital with the intention of making a profit, right? So, are they the same? The distinction is at best blurry. I often pose the question on my Twitter page and, even with the 36,000 followers I have (bots included), I don't really get a definitive answer.

Some say, "Investing is long term." I'd say what about short-term traders? Others will say the differentiator is "skill and knowledge". Are you telling me someone betting on horse racing doesn't research their picks and has no aptitude? I'm happy to argue the point all day, but investing and gambling are fundamentally the same thing. You put up capital in the hope to make more (and lose none).

For me, any investment or gamble comes down to risk, structure and expectations – as well as continually managing them.

What Do Investors Fear the Most?

When it comes to stock market investing, to obtain a structure, you should really examine what you fear most (a point that applies to any form of gambling). Depending on their situation and the state of the market, investors can experience a variety of worries. Below are five common worries. Being aware of them can help build your structure and confidence, and ultimately manage your investments.

1. Loss of principal: Naturally, investors worry about losing their initial investment. The fear of losing their hard-earned money can be a major issue, whether it is because of poor investment decisions, market downturns or unforeseen situations.
2. Market volatility: Investors frequently worry about abrupt, dramatic market changes that could cause considerable losses. It can be challenging to forecast and plan for investing outcomes in volatile markets.
3. Geopolitical events: Uncertainty in the market can be brought on by geopolitical events such as political unrest, war or trade issues. Investors worry that such events could cause market falls, destabilize economies and have an influence on business operations.
4. Economic recession: Investors might be concerned about a generalized economic downturn, such as a financial crisis or recession. These may have a negative effect on investment performance across many industries and asset classes.
5. Black Swan Events: These are unforeseen, infrequent occurrences that can have serious repercussions and disrupt financial markets and investments. Examples include terrorism, pandemics, natural disasters and other unplanned shocks.

Individual investors will have varying levels of worry depending on their risk tolerance and financial goals; it's crucial to keep this in mind. Investors' fears also will change over time, so understanding what you fear most at any stage in time is a very important element of risk-managing your investments.

CHAPTER 1

Things an Investor Should Avoid When Investing

Stock market investing can be profitable, but there are hazards involved. Investors need to be aware of the potential dangers and steer clear of common mistakes to increase their chances of success.

Looking back, not thoroughly doing my research in the early years resulted in some very poor investment decisions. Lack of research at the expense of quick profits must be the number one thing to avoid for any potential entry. Jumping into a stock without doing due diligence is one of the biggest blunders investors can make.

Poor investment selections can result from a failure to comprehend a company's fundamentals, financial health, competitive environment, and industry developments. Investors should spend time studying a company's financials, annual reports, market conditions and management's past performance. The risk of investing in companies with unstable business models or expensive equities rises when research is neglected. Never enter an investment without doing your homework and certainly never rely on someone else's homework either.

Trading on emotion is the second area where most investors go wrong. You'll be surprised to learn that emotion can drive investment decisions for new and seasoned investors.

Emotions have the potential to impair reason and cause irrational behavior. During market downturns, greed and anxiety can drive investors to chase lucrative trends or lose control. Impulsive responses to short-term market changes may lead to purchases at inflated prices or sales during transient declines.

It is crucial to establish a disciplined investment strategy, adhere to a long-term plan, and refrain from making snap judgments based on passing market turbulence. As I often say to people, buy into any company as if you are an owner of the business long term.

Timing the markets is touted as a skill with investing, but it should never be practiced – it really is a waste of time. In my 35 years of being in the market, I have never met anyone who can consistently time the market to their benefit. It's dangerous to try to time the market or engage in speculative trading. Even for seasoned pros, attempting to predict the precise peaks and troughs of the market is extremely difficult and has huge opportunity cost too.

In the same way, speculative trading prioritizes recent price changes over underlying fundamentals. Instead of concentrating on short-term market timing or speculative trades that depend on luck rather than well-informed decision making, investors should aim for a long-term strategy that emphasizes the quality of investments. Again, having the mindset of a long-term owner will help a great deal here.

Putting all your hard-earned cash on black, to use a gambling metaphor, is likely to be a losing strategy. Concentration risk is increased when all your money is put into one stock or a small selection of equities. A single unfavorable occurrence or subpar performance of a particular company might have a big effect on the investment portfolio.

Investments should be dispersed throughout a variety of sectors, industries and asset classes to reduce risk. By diversifying, investors might profit from strong market performance while reducing their exposure to the volatility of specific companies.

Personally, I am the opposite. I prefer to take 10–15 positions based on deep research into each company, though diversification for a lot of investors will limit and spread your risk. I don't think the work involved is any less but it will cushion the impact of any large adverse movement to your portfolio and give you a slight margin of safety if you missed anything in your research.

Don't Forget the Negatives

So, you have your position and you're ready to take that huge return down the road. Wait, You forgot to identify the bad aspects of the investment. Investors are at risk of suffering big losses if risk management is neglected. The various risks connected with investments, such as market risks, industry risks, company-specific risks, and geopolitical risks, must be identified and evaluated. Applying risk management tactics like stop-loss orders, position sizing guidelines or hedging strategies can reduce negative risk.

Investors should also make sure they have adequate liquidity reserves or an emergency fund to handle unforeseen financial difficulties. Furthermore, it's very important to put these risk controls in *before* you enter the investment. As I always say, start with risk.

Something I see regularly, all over social media, are tipsters – and it's not only social media. Recommendations of companies to buy because you've heard it's a winner from your friend or colleague are a huge no. Do not do this at any cost, no matter how solid and convincing the story is. The chances that you and your friends know something that the market doesn't and that isn't priced into the share price are extremely remote to say the least.

Without enough research, relying on hot tips, rumors or market frenzy will only lead to disappointment. Promotional efforts, social media chitchat or insider information can cause stock values to briefly jump but quickly plummet. Investment prospects must be carefully considered based on solid research, fundamental analysis and trustworthy sources of information. Making financial decisions based solely on hearsay can result in big losses and tarnish your reputation. More importantly, it can knock your confidence.

I've said it a few times now and I'll hammer it home once more. Act like an owner when you buy a company's stock. Even if the returns are realized sooner, act with a long-term view and objective. Constantly buying and selling stocks to generate quick money can lead to higher transaction costs, higher taxes and missed possibilities for compounding gains. Patience and discipline are necessary for successful investing. You can weather short-term turbulence and gain from the benefits of time and compound growth by concentrating on long-term objectives.

Stock market investing needs restraint and self-control. Investors can improve their odds of long-term market success by avoiding common mistakes like incomplete research, emotional decision making, a lack of diversification and speculative trading.

How the Structure of Your Investment Should Look

Believe it or not, most investors can pick stocks. It's the lack of structure and process that is usually the killer when things don't go to plan. The ultimate path to value can be railroaded by several different factors. Understanding your investment is the key to either seeing it through or exiting it at a time that won't cause you significant loss.

An investment's primary process normally includes several crucial steps, from preliminary research and analysis through to continuing monitoring and review. The specific procedures may vary based on the type of investment and the investor's unique situation.

As we've identified, many investors consider capital preservation to be one of their main objectives. To prevent severe losses that can imperil the initial investment, risk management and assessment are essential. Investors can make better judgments and preserve their cash by being aware of the potential hazards involved. This boils down to risk.

The number one thing you should start with before you enter an investment is risk. This contrasts with most other investors, who start with upside or P&L. A crucial component of investing is considering risk, since it will enable you to make well-informed choices, control your expectations and match your investment plan to your risk appetite. I'm passionate about investors ensuring risk is managed, so we're going to spend a little time on that topic here. It ideally should be 80% of your process. It is for me. Here is how I go about it and what I look for.

In investment, risk and return are frequently associated. Higher potential profits on investments frequently come with higher degrees of risk. Investors can choose investments that are in line with their desired rate of return and risk tolerance by comprehending and assessing the risks related to various types of investments.

Every investor has a different level of risk tolerance, which refers to their disposition and their capacity to put up with changes in the value of their holdings. While some investors are more risk-averse and favor lower-risk investments, others might feel more at ease taking on greater amounts of risk in the hopes of earning possibly bigger returns. Investors can determine their risk tolerance and make investing choices accordingly by starting with risk.

Assessing the risks associated with an investment opportunity requires conducting research and due diligence. By starting with risk, you are encouraged to gather information and analyze factors such as market conditions, financial statements, industry trends, and regulatory environment. This research will help you make more informed decisions and better understand the potential risks you may face. You should ultimately have your own trusted sources or ways of doing this.

To ask the question again, is this a focused investment or part of a diversified portfolio? Spreading investments over several asset classes, industries and geographical areas is a risk management method known as diversification. You can lessen the effect of a single investment's bad performance on the entire portfolio by diversifying. You can take risk into account by assessing the risk exposures in your portfolio and change the way the assets are allocated to achieve diversification and reduce risk.

You can control your emotions more effectively during times of market volatility or unexpected developments by being aware of and recognizing the risks involved. Starting with risk encourages investors to adopt a disciplined approach to investing, decreasing the likelihood that you will act rashly out of fear or greed.

When creating a long-term investment plan, risk assessment is crucial. You can develop reasonable expectations and set attainable goals by taking risk considerations into account. Select investing methods that fit your long-term ambitions and financial objectives by being aware of the dangers.

It's crucial to understand that risk in investments cannot be completely removed. However, you can make better decisions, create an appropriate investment strategy and manage your money successfully by starting with risk.

Final Areas to Consider

The evaluation of risk will get you most of the way there. Using this knowledge and structure is a continuous process which you must practice again and again until it's engrained. Start by writing it down. Keep tabs on your investments' performance, the state of the market and any pertinent news or events that might have an influence on your holdings. Monitor important indicators, examine financial statements and assess how your investments are doing in relation to your objectives.

To maintain the correct asset allocation, assess and rebalance your investment portfolio on a regular basis. This may involve adjusting to reflect shifting market conditions, risk tolerance or investment objectives. Rebalancing entails buying or selling investments to get the asset mix back to where it should be. Try not to let one position become too large if it's going in your favor.

Lastly, compare the performance of your investment portfolio to the goals you've set. Examine results, compare them to chosen benchmarks and consider any changes or enhancements your investing strategy may require. Future investment decisions are made more informed by this analysis.

It's crucial to understand that the investment process is not linear and that several stages may overlap or call for revisiting at different points. Having a systematic investment process has many advantages, but it's vital to remember that there are still risks involved in investing, and no strategy can ensure success.

Your behavior is disciplined by a systematic investment procedure.

It promotes adhering to the specified investment strategy, refraining from rash purchases or sales, and keeping a long-term perspective. Investors who practice disciplined investing are better able to keep focused on their objectives and resist being seduced by market commotion or transient volatility.

Finally, as Warren Buffett points out, "Risk comes from not knowing what you're doing."

CHAPTER 2

Introduction to Stock Special Situations and Spin-offs

- → What Are Special Situations & Spin-offs?
- → The Potential of Special Situations in Investment
- → Advantages and Risks of Investing in Special Situations
- → Why Spin-offs & Special Situations Present Unique Investment Opportunities

Introduction to Stock Special Situations and Spin-offs

THIS BOOK IS about special situations and spin-offs in stocks, which create opportunities for investors. I refer to special situations as catalysts because these events lead to a change in the stock price of the company. I explain this in more detail in this chapter.

But I'd like to begin this chapter with a story about Toys "R" Us. The story of this company is illustrative of a position that investors often find themselves in.

Toys "R" Us

Toys "R" Us was once a dominant player in the toy retail industry. In my era at least, we all shopped there at some stage. In the 1990s, Toys "R" Us was at its peak. It was the world's largest toy retailer at the time, with over 1,450 outlets in 37 countries. The firm controlled a quarter of the global toy market. It was an experience to go there. It was known for its friendly staff and wide selection of toys. The locations were accessible and the goal of the founder, Charles Lazarus, in 1948, was to make a one stop shop for all things toys. He succeeded in his vision.

Toys "R" Us began to struggle in the 2000s. Incurring huge debt was a major contributor to the demise of the company. Since being acquired by private equity in 2005, the company's leverage had steadily increased. The company's financial flexibility was constrained because of the leveraged buyout's addition of significant debt to the balance sheet.

E-commerce was also an issue. As the digital age developed, websites such as Amazon became increasingly popular. Toys "R" Us had a tough time adapting to the rise of internet shopping since it had not made sufficient investments in its own e-commerce infrastructure.

The company also faced increased competition from discount warehouse clubs like Walmart and Target, which carried a wider variety of goods, including toys. Toys "R" Us saw its market share steadily erode because of competition from stores offering identical toys at lower rates.

As shopping centers encountered problems and consumer habits shifted, fewer people shopped at physical locations. Toys "R" Us was particularly vulnerable to the rise of online shopping as its business strategy was highly dependent on the performance of its physical stores.

The company failed to adapt to the expectations of its customers because its retail design was too rigid. Their enormous store formats failed to meet customers' demands for more engaging and exciting shopping experiences, which were met by competitors. Inadequate online presence and e-commerce capabilities compared to those of its rivals was indicative of a weak digital strategy. Because of this, it had a hard time competing in the expanding e-commerce sector.

Lastly, children's interests were evolving from traditional toys to digital media and technological devices, reflecting a trend in consumer culture. Toys "R" Us had a hard time adjusting to the new environment.

Toys "R" Us saw a huge decline in sales and income because of these issues, which led to financial strain. A Chapter 11 bankruptcy petition was filed by the corporation in September 2017 to reorganize debt and continue operations. Despite best attempts, the company could not find its footing. The once-great toy store chain decided to shut down operations in the US and the UK.

Cheap for a Reason

A problem that many investors have is that they focus too much on what they think a company is worth, especially its cheapness. They overlook the fact that some companies are cheap for a reason.

It's the same in life. You get what you pay for. This could be a house that is cheap, which may need a lot of work doing to it, a used car with high mileage, or a damaged second-hand item. Life and markets price things pretty much efficiently. Very occasionally something is mispriced. Taking this opportunity is a great excuse to brag to your friends. We've all done it.

There are plenty of cheap companies out there. Investors buy them and wonder why the stock price doesn't go up. When I identify a company that appears to be good value at its current stock price, I first ask myself why is it cheap? There could be multiple reasons for a company being cheap, but I have listed five of the most common below. Toys "R" Us was a great example of a company that was cheap and became cheaper and it ticked many of these boxes:

- **Fundamental weakness:** Stocks that have basic weaknesses, like bad financial performance, falling sales, or a lot of debt, might have trouble attracting investors and, as a result, see their prices grow slowly, not at all, or even decline.
- **Low market interest:** Stocks from certain industries or sectors may be less desirable than others. Stocks in certain sectors may have trouble gaining traction if they are experiencing difficulties or have limited growth possibilities.
- **Conglomerate discounts:** Lack of focus, company complexity, difficulty in valuation, and risks across a variety of sectors can cause a company's stock price to remain subdued.
- **Strategic direction:** Lack of a focused and coherent business strategy is often the result of poor management decisions. Strong leadership that can guide the company to expansion and profitability is highly valued by investors.

- **Investor sentiment:** Sometimes a company is viewed as not being part of the future and in a tech-driven environment, these types of names can be left behind by investors. Alternatively, a cyclical industry, say retail, might not be viewed as performing in a recession.

So, you have your valuation that is cheap, and you have established why it's cheap. The decision to then buy the company is a trap that a lot of investors fall into. Something that is cheap will not necessarily go up. News about a particular company can worsen and cheap can become cheaper. See Toys "R" Us!

Price Catalysts

A catalyst for a stock is an event that could have a big effect on the price and volume of trading in that stock. These are often known as special situations, because it's a new (or special!) situation developing at the company.

Catalysts can be either good or bad, and they often have a big impact on how investors feel and how the market moves. They can be anything from company-specific events to broader trends in the economy or a certain business. The important point to remember here is that catalysts can move a company's stock price toward its true value. Whenever I make a new investment, I am looking for a catalyst that is going to move the stock price in my favor.

Catalysts are broken down into soft and hard versions. The key difference lies in the degree of certainty and immediacy of their impact on the stock's price.

Let's look at soft and hard catalysts in turn.

Soft Catalysts

A soft catalyst is an event or factor that has an indirect or gradual impact on the price of a company. It may not have an immediate and decisive impact on the stock's value, and its impact may be more difficult to forecast. Soft catalysts are frequently associated with broader market trends, investor mood, or qualitative issues. Industry developments, macroeconomic considerations, shifting customer tastes, and shifts in investor opinion are all examples.

A soft catalyst, for example, may be a company's choice to increase its sustainability efforts if there is a growing trend of corporations adopting environmentally friendly practices. While this may not result in an immediate price increase, it may have a good impact on the investor view of the company's long-term prospects. Soft catalysts include:

- A rise in earnings is a common and relatively minor stimulus. A company's stock price may rise once it publishes earnings that exceed market expectations.
- The introduction of a brand-new product is another example of a soft catalyst. A company's stock price might rise if the public embraces a newly released product, which in turn boosts the company's revenue and earnings.
- Another example of a softer catalyst is a change in leadership. An increase in the stock price may follow the hiring of a new CEO who has a history of success.
- A soft catalyst could also be a positive review from an analyst. An upgrade in a stock's rating from a major investment bank might be a signal to buyers that the stock is underpriced and a good buy.
- Increased investor interest could also play a supporting role. Investor interest is a key factor in a stock's price appreciation.

Hard Catalysts

A hard catalyst is a precise, concrete event that has an immediate and direct impact on the price of a company. These incidents are frequently easier to foresee and have more immediate consequences. Earnings reports, product launches, regulatory clearances, mergers and acquisitions, dividend announcements, and stock buybacks are examples of hard catalysts.

Once a pharmaceutical business gets regulatory approval for a new drug, it becomes a difficult catalyst since it can produce an instantaneous and significant change in the company's earning potential, therefore generating volatility. Driven by market responses to the expected income from the new drug, this is resulting from possible fast changes in investor expectations and stock price.

In essence, the primary distinction between a soft and a hard stock catalyst is the level of immediacy and predictability of the impact on stock prices. Soft catalysts have a slower and more uncertain impact, whereas hard catalysts have a clear, direct, and often instantaneous impact on the value of a company.

- Mergers, acquisitions, and takeover announcements can cause major price changes. The stock price of one or both companies involved may be influenced depending on how the market interprets the impact of the transaction.
- Receiving regulatory clearance for new products or medical treatments can have an immediate beneficial influence on stock prices for companies in industries such as pharmaceuticals or biotechnology.
- When a firm declares a dividend rise, it frequently implies financial health and investor-friendly policies, which can lead to increased demand and higher stock prices.
- A company spin-off is the result of a parent firm distributing shares of a subsidiary to its employees, therefore generating a new, autonomous company. This might affect the stock price since it usually causes the parent and the spun-off firm to realign their worth.
- Other business acts that modify the company's structure. Exchange offers, split-offs, restructuring business units, reverse mergers, divestitures, reorganizations, and capital structure modifications are examples of these. This can significantly impact stock prices by changing the company's financial outlook and market position.

The Potential of Special Situations in Investing

Hopefully you are beginning to see the two-stage process here. First, identify the reason for the stock being cheap; and second, find the catalyst that will move its price to value. With these two points, you can start to find some powerful reasons for investing your money in good quality companies. Combine this with your process and you'll be smarter than most of your peers.

Let's now have a more detailed introductory look at the most important types of special situations, before we move on to cover these in the rest of the book.

Arbitrage in Mergers and Acquisitions (M&A)

When businesses announce mergers or acquisitions, the stock price of the target company may not accurately represent the offer price. Investors can purchase shares of the target firm below the offer price and make money once the acquisition is closed.

The "discount" on the price is a combination of time value until the deal closes and the probability of it closing. You are playing for a very small amount of money. This is why sophisticated investors do it in huge size.

The risk of these types of investments is that a break of the deal will cause a huge loss and negate the many small profits from previous deals. The risk-reward isn't there for me, but some can do it successfully if their timing proves correct.

Spin-offs

When a company spins off a subsidiary or division as a separate entity, it can lead to mispricing and undervaluation of the spun-off company. Investors who recognize the potential of the spun-off entity can benefit from its growth prospects.

These are my favorite investments and I have dedicated a whole chapter to them. If you carry out enough work here, these can be lucrative investments that can give you abnormal returns. Risks can be easily quantified and are less inclined to be influenced by outside forces.

Distressed Securities

Investing in distressed companies that are facing financial difficulties can yield significant returns if the company successfully restructures and recovers. However, this type of investment involves higher risk.

View the company like you knew someone who was in high debt. What are the chances of them getting out of their debt? Should they borrow more money and refinance? Should they hire someone (new management?), or just change direction and work smarter?

Investing in distressed companies can be risky. If things don't get better, a distressed company might not succeed in turning things around. So, people who invest in these situations need to be careful and do a lot of research to understand if it's a good idea. These situations can be very lucrative if the firm turns around.

Bankruptcy and Restructuring

Companies undergoing bankruptcy or financial restructuring may offer opportunities for investors who can accurately assess the potential outcomes and recovery values of the company's assets. This is a type of distressed investing. Usually, the solution is an investor coming in to provide finance.

Now, here's where it gets interesting. Some people who are good at understanding business and money might see an opportunity in this situation. They might decide to invest their own money in the bankrupt company. Usually, these people or institutions are astute and can see things others don't.

It's good practice to look at their success on past deals. Investing with them gives you a higher probability of success, but ensure you do your own work too. Investing in a bankrupt company is taking a big risk. Just like your indebted friend, they might not bounce back and make money again. A bankrupt company might not be able to turn things around, so these situations become an extremely high-risk, high-reward bet.

Rights Offerings

When companies offer existing shareholders the right to buy additional shares at a discounted price, investors can potentially profit by taking advantage of the discounted share price.

Imagine that you own stock in a corporation and are one of its shareholders. Let's imagine this business needs to raise more capital to expand, or pay off debts. The business decides to ask its current shareholders if they want to invest extra money, instead of the company borrowing money from banks or other sources.

An offering of rights can help in this situation. As a current shareholder, you have a unique privilege known as a "subscription right". It functions as a kind of invitation to purchase additional shares of the company's stock at a price that is lower than the going market rate.

While taking part in a rights offering can have benefits, it's crucial to understand the dangers involved. The possibility to expand ownership at a cheaper cost can be offered by the discounted price, but there is still a chance that the stock price will change during the subscription period, possibly resulting in immediate paper losses. Your ability to purchase more shares may be restricted by oversubscription, which happens when there are more shareholders seeking to join than there are shares available. This will affect your ownership percentage.

Furthermore, the issuance of additional shares may reduce the ownership of current shareholders, reducing their relative ownership of the company. The value of the newly purchased shares may also be impacted by the company's uncertain future performance.

Additionally, taking part in a rights offering holds up money, thereby preventing you from taking advantage of other, better investment options. Your returns may also be impacted by how management uses the funding received and the success of the company's post-offering activities.

Important factors to consider are the announcement's effect on the market mood and the constrained window of opportunity for decision making. To help you make an informed decision, the company must provide accurate and comprehensive information on the justifications for the offer, its plans for the money collected, and the future prospects of the business.

In essence, even while rights offers might offer the option to increase ownership and acquire shares at a discount, careful assessment of these possible risks in the context of the company's financial health and prospects is crucial for making wise investment decisions.

Activist Investing

Activist investing is acquiring a sizeable position in a company's stock with the goal of exerting influence and bringing about changes inside the organization to increase shareholder value. Activist investors actively promote certain policies, changes, or strategic alterations to enhance the organization's financial performance, corporate governance, operational effectiveness, and total market value.

This approach entails engaging in direct discussions, public letters, proxy battles, and other means to convey recommendations to company management and boards of directors. The overarching objective is to identify opportunities for greater efficiency, improved financial performance, and increased competitiveness, all with the aim of benefiting shareholders.

The strategies of activist investors can vary, encompassing both short-term-focused efforts, such as advocating for share buybacks, and long-term strategies that emphasize sustainable growth through broader structural changes.

While successful activist campaigns can yield considerable returns for both activists and other shareholders, potential challenges include conflicts with existing management, market volatility due to campaign announcements, and the complexity of implementing proposed changes.

Consequently, investors exploring activist strategies should conduct thorough due diligence, consider the potential implications of advocated changes, and assess the alignment of an activist's intentions with the long-term health of the targeted company before making investment decisions.

On the face of it, an activist firm with prior experience of creating value can be viewed as a good thing and why shouldn't you just go ahead and invest with them?

But investors should carefully assess the inherent dangers of investing with activists. As a result of activist efforts that question current leadership and tactics, disputes with the firm management can occur. This fight may cause disruption and uncertainty in the company's day-to-day business operations, which may influence the stock price.

Activists' goals are aligned with the interests of shareholders; therefore, they may fight for changes that endanger the company's long-term potential and ultimately negate what they initially set out to achieve.

Furthermore, activist actions can cause short-term market volatility, causing stock values to change as investors respond to announcements made during activist campaigns. It's also crucial to keep in mind that activist-driven improvements can take time to implement and aren't always successful, which might leave investors disappointed.

Finally, a business that has been singled out by activists may devote significant resources to resisting the campaign, detracting from its primary activities, and possibly harming overall performance. These dangers serve as a reminder to investors that before engaging in activist-driven investments, they should properly investigate the motivations of the activists, examine the viability and long-term impact of proposed methods, and determine whether these strategies are consistent with their own investment goals.

Changes in How a Company Raises and Manages its Cash

The last area I want to highlight is when there are significant changes in how a company raises and manages its funds. This can transform a company's capital structure. These occurrences frequently influence a company's debt and equity mix, which affects the stability of its finances and overall worth.

Examples of important transactions that can result in the issuing of new shares or debt to fund the transaction include mergers and acquisitions (M&A). When distinct businesses are formed through a spin-off, the capitalization of both the parent business and the newly formed subsidiary may vary. Equity offers, like initial public offerings (IPOs) and secondary offerings, change equity composition by introducing new shares to the market.

Debt obligations and financing costs for the company are impacted by the issuing or refinancing of debt, including bond offerings or convertible debt. Share buybacks or repurchases decrease the number of outstanding shares, which could increase stock prices and change ownership ratios.

Finally, changes such as dividend increases or decreases have an impact on how the company allocates its resources and attracts income-seeking investors.

Each of these occurrences is an example of a strategic decision that can alter a company's financial structure, risk profile, cost of capital, and investor appeal.

Conclusion

To sum up, spin-offs and unusual circumstances provide investors with a different lens through which they can unearth hidden wealth and exploit chances amid market upheavals. They present a compelling opportunity for those prepared to handle the complexity, seize the potential rewards, and comprehend the associated hazards because of their distinctive qualities, the potential for significant returns, and alignment with particular investment strategies.

In the next chapter, we move on to look at the fundamentals of how to look at a company through the eyes of special situations.

CHAPTER 3

Identifying Stock Special Situations and Spin-offs

- Identifying Opportunities in Special Situations
- Analytical Tools and Techniques
- Risk Management and Diversification
- Building a Special Situations and Spin-offs Investment Strategy

OVER THE COURSE of my career in stock market analysis, I've become an expert in the nuances of unique situations and spin-offs, two areas rich with untapped potential that any astute investor can exploit. Mergers, acquisitions, restructurings and even bankruptcy situations are all examples of special events that might lead to the discovery of stocks that are momentarily underpriced because of business turmoil or market reactions.

Special situations and spin-offs are attractive investment options because they can help diversify a portfolio and reduce exposure to market fluctuations, in addition to the large rewards they may provide. In these cases, investors need to be experts at deciphering intricate company stories to find hidden opportunities to unlock value that the market is blind to. As an example, smart investors can profit from a re-rating that occurs when a spin-off is implemented since it causes a reassessment of the parent and offspring's actual worth.

Investors who are skilled at navigating these waters have a leg up in the market since it allows them to diversify their holdings and gain access to companies that are heading for a resurgence. Honing one's aptitude in this specialized financial arena is crucial – attuning oneself to the tiny indications that highlight these chances.

Identifying Opportunities in Special Situations

Identifying the special situation can often come down to just reading a lot or alternatively screening. I do both. To find opportunities for investing in unique situations, you need to be able to read both obvious and subtle signs that point to hidden value waiting to be found. I've learned to rely on a mix of financial metrics and qualitative indicators over the years. They help me find my way through the often confusing news of company changes and market shifts.

The main part is the study of financial metrics. One important metric is the EBITDA margin, which shows how well a company is running in a certain situation. A big jump in this number after the news of a reorganization or split can point to a leaner, more focused business ready to make money.

Also, looking at the price-to-earnings (P/E) ratio compared to other companies in the same business can show valuation differences that need more research. Effects on earnings per share (EPS) that increase or decrease give a number representation of the possible value that will be gained or lost from a merger or other corporate action.

Along with the numbers, qualitative measures are also very important. The strategic reason for a sale, spin-off, or restructuring can help put the numbers in context. For example, it might be to get rid of non-core assets, lower debt, or take advantage of growth possibilities in a new company.

Changes in leadership, especially the hiring of executives who have been through similar problems before, are often the first step toward a successful turnaround or the discovery of hidden value. A great example of this is when Larry Culp took over General Electric in 2018. He brought the business back from near bankruptcy and created huge value by splitting up the divisions.

Also, the way the market reacts right after a statement about a special situation can give clues, even if they are based on speculation. Overreaction that leads to an unnecessary sell-off is a chance to buy, while market indifference might mean that you need to dig deeper to find value that you missed. You will find that these methods are moving targets. When companies become cheap, focus more on the metrics, and when companies are more fairly priced, focus on the value creative part due to the corporate action.

These financial metrics and qualitative indicators work together to create a complete framework for finding possible winners in the complicated world of special situations. To successfully handle the complex aspects of these one-of-a-kind business opportunities, you must master this framework, which you can only do by practicing and always learning.

Financial Analysis for Spin-offs and Special Situations

Successfully maneuvering through the intricate realm of spin-offs and other corporate actions demands a combination of expert knowledge and meticulous analysis. I have developed a strong reliance on three key financial metrics: EBITDA, the P/E ratio and debt analysis. These metrics serve as invaluable guides to finding hidden value and potential risks.

EBITDA is like the engine under the hood of a company. It strips away all the financial bells and whistles, leaving you with a clear picture of how efficiently they're turning their core business into cash. This is especially crucial when looking at spin-offs. You want to understand if the new company can stand on its own two feet, and EBITDA gives you a great starting point. It can help uncover hidden gems within a larger corporation – businesses that were overshadowed but have the potential to thrive independently.

The P/E ratio, when compared to sector averages, serves as an indicator of market valuation and sentiment. Irregularities in this ratio, particularly following announcements of unique circumstances, frequently indicate undervalued assets – opportunities where the market has not yet fully acknowledged a company's true value after a transition.

Fully understanding a company's debt exposure can provide key insights into its financial strength. After a spin-off or restructuring, it is important for a company to have a sustainable or reduced debt level.

This indicates their ability to strategically navigate and grow, which is essential for taking advantage of opportunities after the transition.

These analytical foundations, developed over many years, are more than just tools – they serve as a guide for understanding the complex dynamics of unique circumstances. They empower a seasoned market participant to navigate through the clutter, pinpointing those unique opportunities where the market's perception has not yet aligned with reality – where genuine value lies in wait for the astute and patient investor.

Technical Analysis, Research and Data

Having a deep understanding of the intricacies of investing is vital for success. Mastering the art of timing is crucial in navigating delicate circumstances, but don't let this be your sole focus. It's where expertise in unique circumstances becomes your secret weapon. It's not a foolproof solution, but is a valuable tool for navigating the unpredictable terrain of entry and exit. But be warned – it can also be a pitfall. Here are the tools I use.

Understanding chart patterns: Consider these as the market's hidden code. Those patterns on a chart are more than just random lines. They provide valuable insights into investor sentiment, offering hints about possible price fluctuations. For example, in a spin-off, a breakout from a tight consolidation pattern may indicate increasing confidence and an imminent upswing. It's important to consider entering early to avoid the crowd.

Volume analysis: Picture volume as the pulse of the market. A significant price movement with minimal trading activity is akin to a feeble pulse – its longevity may be questionable. But an unexpected increase in trading activity accompanied by a significant price movement? That's a strong and confident heartbeat, indicating a true belief in the market's direction. When it comes to unique special situations, where investor sentiment can be unpredictable, analyzing volume can help distinguish temporary fluctuations from meaningful trends.

Momentum indicators: Think of these as the essential tools for your investing endeavors. They analyze the velocity of price fluctuations and indicate whether there is excessive activity (possibly caused by a surge in buying) or a decline in momentum. In particularly unpredictable spin-offs, these indicators can be incredibly helpful. For instance, a situation where the relative strength index (RSI) is oversold could suggest a temporary decline following the spin-off, which could potentially be seen as a favorable time to consider buying.

Again, always keep in mind that technical analysis serves as a guide, rather than a precise navigation system. It provides guidance based on historical patterns and market sentiment, but unexpected events are always a possibility. That's why conducting thorough research is essential.

Exploring data and research platforms: There are fantastic resources out there to bolster your research on spin-offs and special situations. Websites such as Capital IQ, S&P Capital IQ and FactSet provide extensive databases containing financial data, news and company filings. However, I don't rely on just these. Setting up screens with keywords of what you are looking for is also essential if you are going to capture the wider landscape.

Risk Management and Diversification

I've improved several tactics over the years to lower these risks and make sure that my search for value doesn't leave my portfolio too open to harm.

Diversifying your portfolio: Diversification is an important part of managing risk, and it's especially important when there are special cases or spin-offs. Spreading investments across different industries, asset types and even locations makes the effect of a single bad event much smaller. This method not only lowers risk, but it also sets up the portfolio to take advantage of a wider range of chances by balancing possible high-risk, high-reward investments with safer, lower-return assets.

Stop-loss orders: Stop-loss orders are an important way to protect capital in special situations and spin-offs, where things can change quickly. Investors can limit their losses on any given investment by setting a price level below which the position will be instantly sold. This mechanism is especially helpful for handling the unpredictability that comes with these sectors. It acts as a great safety net that keeps short-term market drops from hurting the portfolio in the long run. It's important to have them, but be prepared, they can hurt.

Continuous monitoring and adaptation: In addition to these tactical steps, it is important to keep a constant eye on the investment landscape and be ready to change strategies in response to new risks. This is the only way to handle special situations and spin-offs successfully. This means keeping your news flow targeted on market trends, changes in regulations and news about the company, and being ready to switch course or reallocate resources as needed. By doing this you not only lower your risk but also take advantage of new chances that come up, because the market is always changing.

It's clear that special situations and spin-offs are appealing, but they also come with big and complicated risks. Investors can get through these problems, though, if they take a careful approach to risk management that includes diversifying their portfolios, using stop-loss orders strategically, keeping a close eye on things, and being flexible. This allows you to pursue the unique opportunities these sectors offer while maintaining a strong defense against the risks they come with. If you take this balanced method, looking for big returns in unique situations and spin-offs can be both fun and safe.

Patience and Timing

When it comes to taking advantage of business opportunities in unique situations and spin-offs, you can't overemphasize the importance of patience and timing. These chances usually arise at times that don't match up perfectly with what the market or investors want, which is where patience comes in.

It's not initially always clear when to join or exit these investments. You need to know how the markets work and be patient until the right time comes along. You can handle risk and volatility by making sure that actions are timed perfectly to match strategic goals and ideal market conditions. Patience and timing turn potential worth into real gains. This is how the waiting game can be used as a strategic advantage.

Building a Special Situations and Spin-offs Investment Strategy

A thorough familiarity with peculiar situations and spin-offs, as well as a strategic approach to managing them, are prerequisites for developing a solid investment plan that is adapted to specific terrain. This starts with a comprehensive due diligence process that makes use of financial indicators, market analysis and a deep understanding of the underlying businesses. Nevertheless, the approach does not conclude with investment; it encompasses constant vigilance and a readiness to modify holdings in response to changing market conditions.

As important as it is to carry out continuous study, it is equally critical to monitor changes in regulations, market sentiment and operational developments at the target companies. A method like this keeps the strategy flexible and in line with the original investing thesis, even when faced with unexpected changes. Achieving success in these fields requires not only seeing opportunities, but also painstakingly developing and fine-tuning a plan over time.

Having this capability gives you a leg up in the market by turning the inherent volatility and complexity of unusual situations and spin-offs into a treasure trove of investment opportunities. Investors can take advantage of these one-of-a-kind market events to their fullest extent by following this methodical yet adaptable approach, which transforms the complexities of each circumstance into an opportunity for higher profits.

CHAPTER 4

The Fundamentals of Looking at a Company through Special Situation Eyes

- Start with Risk Not P&L
- What is a Special Situation?
- Valuation Pre-Event and Post-Event
- What Will Move Price to Value?
- Start and End with Risk – A Framework for Investing
- How to Know When You're Wrong

Start with Risk Not P&L

IN ALL ASPECTS of life, if there is a potential reward, you must accept a degree of risk. As humans, we are wired to avoid risk to survive. Most of us would never run across a busy highway to get somewhere faster or cool ourselves in shark-infested waters. Our instinct tells us that our survival would be in jeopardy, the risk too great.

The psychology of risk is very interesting. Our brains observe risk differently. Each bit of information is interpreted differently, hence affecting our decisions. This phenomenon is prevalent in the investing world. It can be witnessed every minute of the trading day. There is a seller for every buyer.

In my early trading days in the dealing room at the bank, a salesman used to shout over to us traders and ask why a stock was moving higher. If we didn't know, we said, flippantly, "more buyers than sellers." It's a dumb example, but this is precisely what moves stocks, with the inverse of course being equally true.

The risk–return trade-off states that the higher the risk, the higher the reward – and vice versa. Using this principle, low levels of uncertainty (risk) are associated with low potential returns and high levels of uncertainty with high potential returns.

But How Do We Measure Risk?

Daniel Kahneman and Amos Tversky, great pioneers in behavioral finance, showed that people who were asked to choose between a certain loss and a gamble, in which they could either lose more money or break even, would tend to choose the double down (that is, gamble to avoid the prospect of losses), a behavior the authors called "loss aversion."

What they ultimately found is that it is investors' tendency to hold losing investments too long and to sell winners too soon. Overconfidence causes investors to hold concentrated portfolios and to trade excessively, behaviors that can destroy wealth. This is a disaster recipe. Behavioral biases are nothing more than a series of complex trade-offs between risk and reward, and you need to understand this when considering an investment.

Metrics like alpha, beta, R-squared, standard deviation, and Sharpe ratio are all sound risk measures for a portfolio, but nimble investors measure the upside against the downside. If the odds are in their favor, they take the trade.

What is a Special Situation?

Special scenario investment (special situations investing) capitalizes on occurrences that dramatically alter a company's valuation for extraordinary returns. Mergers, acquisitions, spin-offs, restructurings, bankruptcies, and corporate reorganizations are examples.

Special situation investors capitalize on pricing inefficiencies or misunderstood valuations caused by these events. To succeed in this field, you must analyze the event, grasp its financial impact and predict market reactions. Investors employ in-depth research and strategic thinking to find opportunities outside of market cycles.

Valuation Pre-Event and Post-Event

Before a special situation event occurs, you should assess the financial health of the company and the potential effects of the event on its operations and market position. This entails conducting a comprehensive analysis of balance accounts, income statements and cash flows, in addition to evaluating potential shifts in market position and industry dynamics. In addition, benchmarking valuations and gauging market sentiment rely heavily on peer comparisons.

After the event, the strategy transitions to incorporating the results into financial projections, attentively observing the market's response to the event and monitoring the performance of the organization. By continuously evaluating pre-event expectations, investors can adapt their strategies in response to observed fluctuations in stock prices and evolving market sentiment. This ensures that decisions made after the event remain in line with the actual performance of the company.

What Will Move Price to Value?

Price to value fluctuations can be influenced by several factors during exceptional circumstances, such as the market's re-evaluation of the firm's prospective earnings capacity following the occurrence, alterations in operational effectiveness and strategic placement. Furthermore, pivotal factors include investor sentiment, market dynamics and the wider economic landscape. As the event progresses and additional data becomes accessible, these elements cumulatively impact investors' assessments and, as a result, the valuation of the organization.

Start and End with Risk – a Framework for Investing

- **Start with the risks:** The first thing that needs to be done is to focus on the risks rather than the possible benefits. Recognize that you naturally don't like taking risks and how that affects the choices you make. To understand behavioral finance, you need to know how psychological factors such as fear of losing money and being too sure of yourself can affect your financial decisions.
- **Know how the market works:** Markets usually work well because prices show all the knowledge that is available. This makes things

hard for people who can consistently produce alpha, but it also opens opportunities for people who can tell the difference between a right and a wrong price.
- **Understand how crowds act and what makes them feel:** It's crucial to be aware of the emotional and mental factors that affect market changes, like herd behavior and FOMO, and how these factors can lead to chances or traps.
- **Get the edge you want:** Think about your unique skills and ideas. Maybe you have specialized knowledge, good analysis skills or a different point of view on market information. To make more sensible decisions about finances, you should be aware of and act on any behavioral biases you may have.
- **Make smart decisions:** Fundamental analysis, knowledge of how the market works and your own personal insights should be used in tandem to make smart choices.
- **Continue to learn and adapt:** Keep up with the latest changes in your industry, and be ready to change your plan when new information comes in.

How to Know When You're Wrong

To figure out when you're wrong about an equity purchase, especially in a unique case, you need to keep a close eye on how it's doing compared to your original thesis. Some key signs are:

- Not meeting the planned financial goals or metrics.
- Changes in the market or the way competitors do business that hurt the company's chances of success.
- Regulatory or legal problems that weren't previously considered.
- Problems with execution or changes in management's plan that are at odds with why you invested in the first place.

Review your thesis often as new information comes in and be ready to change your mind if basic ideas turn out to be wrong.

PART TWO

SPECIAL SITUATIONS IN PRACTICE

CHAPTER 5

What Are Spin-offs and How Do They Create Value?

- What Is a Spin-off?
- Five Reasons They Happen
- Possible Downsides of Spin-offs
- Do Spin-offs Outperform?

What Is a Spin-off?

I WAS SPEAKING AT a conference once on corporate reorganizations and after the speech an investor came up to me and explained that he never really looked at these sorts of events as investable situations, but that he remembered gaining shares of Chipotle (CMG) through owning McDonald's (MCD) back in 2006. He was chuffed when the price of the first public offering (they had two) doubled to $44 from the initial price of $22 on the first day of trading.

Incidentally, the investor I was speaking to sold them on the day and has been kicking himself since. His primary fault was not knowing enough about the transaction and merely reacting to the prompt from his broker. It's better to be lucky than good, of course, but he could have been much luckier.

Chipotle was purchased by McDonald's in 1998, when there were just 16 outlets in the chain. But as Chipotle expanded and changed into a lucrative standalone company with a distinct fast-casual dining concept, McDonald's made the decision to let it run independently.

In the separation, McDonald's divided shares of Chipotle pro rata to its owners at the time. The transaction was called an "exchange offer", where a company offers to exchange its current securities for new securities in order to restructure the equity. What is important to note here is that releasing good-quality businesses as their own standalone entities can involve huge value creation for the company and, ultimately, the investor.

Chipotle, McDonalds, S&P 500 return, rebased to S&P, October 2006 to October 2022

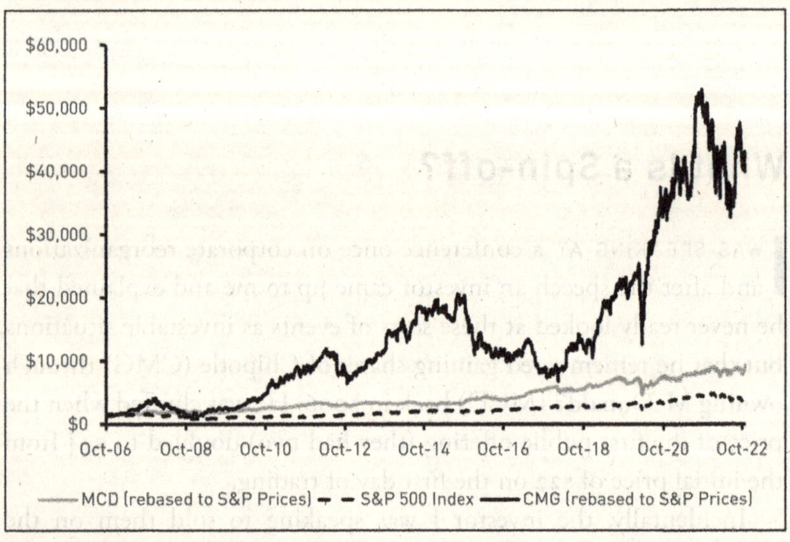

When you have been doing something for as long as I have, you can assume that everyone understands your jargon. But you should remember that what is music to your ears is often a cacophony to others. It took me a long time to remember not to speak in spin-off jargon to potential clients and the masses, and to realize that spin-offs, despite their obvious value to some, are not really that well known.

Corporate spin-offs go by many different names, and terminology might change depending on the situation and location. For example, the process of severing a business unit or division from the parent firm to form a new, independent corporation is referred to as a "demerger" in various places outside the US, particularly in Europe and India.

In a corporate restructuring action known as a "spin-off", a parent company separates one of its business units or divisions to create a freestanding, independent company. By distributing shares of the spun-off company to the parent firm's current owners, two distinct publicly listed entities are formed. The new business that results from a spin-off is frequently referred to as a "spin-off company".

By enabling the separate companies to concentrate on their core strengths and releasing hidden value in specific business divisions, spin-offs can add value for shareholders. Additionally, it gives investors the choice to put money into various businesses in line with their investing preferences and risk tolerance. Or, for that matter, to remove them.

The media frequently get it wrong when covering spin-offs. This is an important point to remember. A "true" spin-off only happens when a share of a division is distributed amongst existing shareholders that own the parent company. Contrary to what you might hear from the media, IPOs, divestitures, carve-outs, split-offs and split-ups are not spin-offs, and consequently these transactions lose many of the value-creating dynamics of the spin-off corporate action.

In order to fully comprehend the spin-off and its ramifications, investors should cross-reference information from various trustworthy sources, particularly official business statements. They should also look for information from reliable financial analysts, subject-matter experts, and formal regulatory filings, such as those with the Securities and Exchange Commission (SEC).

Five Reasons Spin-offs Happen

Spin-offs happen for a variety of reasons, and it is important to understand what has happened historically and why, so that you can be on the lookout for something similar. Companies generally opt to start a spin-off for specific strategic reasons.

The unique circumstances of the parent company and the business unit being spun off have an impact on each case. A business unit's potential benefits, dangers and effects on both the parent firm and the spun-off corporation are usually evaluated by the auditor ahead of the transaction. Identifying the key reason for a spin-off forms a vital base for your analysis. Many analysts ignore this key and obvious point. It's here where the company is essentially telling you how they are going to create value.

Here are five main reasons companies choose to create spin-offs:

1. Focus and clarity: The parent firm may operate several business units in several sectors, each with its own growth prospects, risk profiles and strategic priorities. For this reason, the firm may want to streamline its operations, generate value and enable each division to independently pursue its distinct strategic goals, by spinning off a particular division. One of the most well-known recent examples of this was the separation of HP Inc. and Hewlett-Packard Enterprise (HPE) from Hewlett-Packard (HP) in November 2015.

Hewlett-Packard

The management of HP realized that the company's numerous business divisions were prohibiting expansion and capacity to successfully compete in a vast range of markets. They had the opinion that, by dividing the companies, each would be able to function independently and concentrate more on its unique core capabilities and market potential.

The purpose of the spin-off was to allow each firm to streamline its operations and make more strategic decisions, while also giving investors clarity and transparency. HP Inc. was the spun-off entity focused on the personal systems and printing businesses. HPE emerged as the separate entity dedicated to enterprise hardware, software and services.

The spin-off provided several benefits to both HP Inc. and HPE:

- **Clarity and responsibility:** By allowing each organization to have its own leadership team, the separation enabled improved responsibility and a focus on certain corporate objectives.

- **Streamlined operations:** With the spin-off, each firm was able to simplify operations, improve operational effectiveness and optimize cost structures.
- **Investor appeal:** Clearer financial reporting and improved insight into each entity's performance were made available to investors, making it simpler for them to assess investment opportunities.
- **Making strategic decisions:** The separate entities were now able to make strategic choices based on their own commercial requirements, market circumstances and growth possibilities.
- **Resources allocation flexibility:** The separation gave each organization the freedom to allocate resources more effectively in accordance with its own business needs and growth aspirations.
- The management of HP Inc. and HPE wanted to make both businesses more competitive, focused and nimble so they could better serve their respective markets and increase shareholder value.

HPQ, HPE, S&P 500 return, rebased to S&P, November 2015 to July 2023

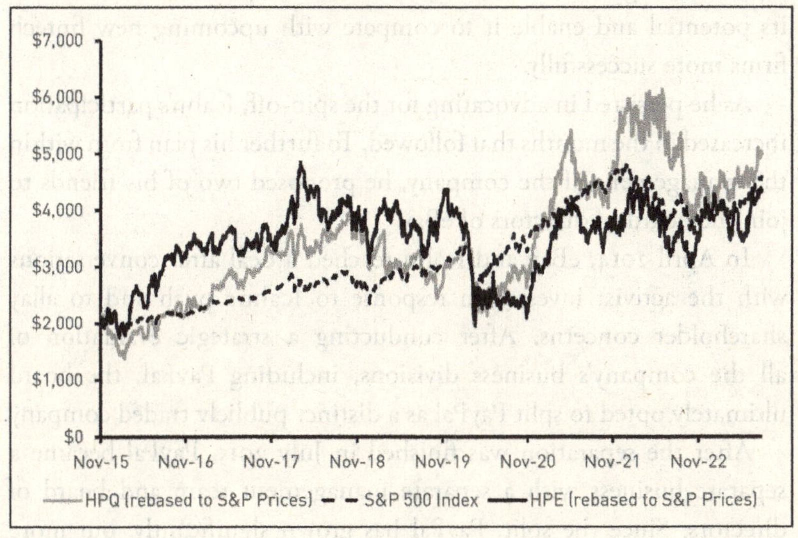

2. Value unlocking/activist pressure: A spin-off can reveal a business unit's hidden value that may not have been fully realized under the conglomerate structure of the parent company. The spun-off corporation may be valued more highly because of independent market evaluation, which would be advantageous to both the parent company and its stockholders.

eBay (EBAY)

In 2014, Carl Icahn, the prominent activist investor, exerted enormous pressure on eBay to separate its PayPal (PYPL) division. Icahn openly demanded that eBay split its e-commerce operation from PayPal in January 2014 after revealing that he had acquired a sizeable investment in the company. He said that the two businesses would be more valuable as separate entities. In the quickly growing digital payment sector, Icahn thought PayPal, as a standalone business, had the potential for faster development and a higher valuation. He stated that detaching PayPal from eBay's e-commerce platform would reveal its potential and enable it to compete with upcoming new fintech firms more successfully.

As he persisted in advocating for the spin-off, Icahn's participation increased in the months that followed. To further his plan from within the management of the company, he proposed two of his friends to join the board of directors of eBay.

In April 2014, eBay and Icahn reached a deal after conversations with the activist investor in response to Icahn's push and to allay shareholder concerns. After conducting a strategic evaluation of all the company's business divisions, including PayPal, the board ultimately opted to split PayPal as a distinct publicly traded company.

After the separation was finished in July 2015, PayPal became a separate business with a separate management team and board of directors. Since the split, PayPal has grown significantly, but more recently, in the last two years, it has run into trouble, as other providers have encroached into their market.

PayPal, ebay, S&P 500 return, rebased to S&P, July 2015 to July 2023

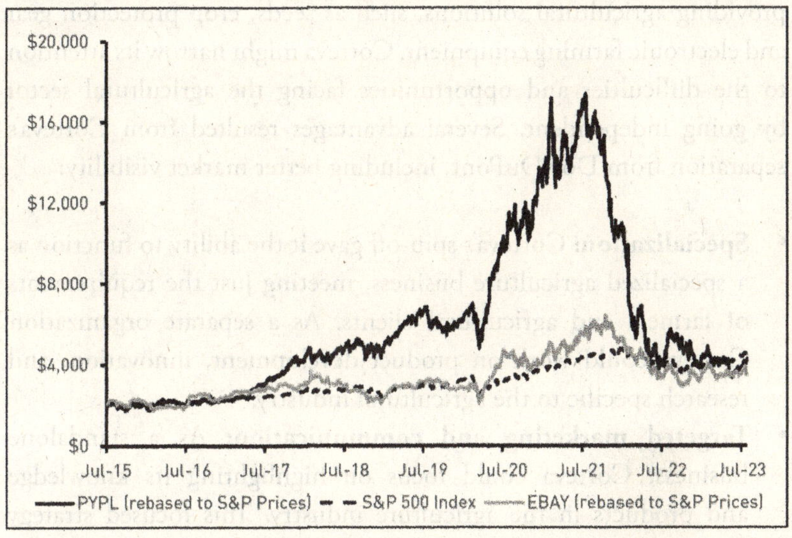

3. **Increased market visibility:** Investors and analysts frequently pay closer attention to smaller, independent businesses. A spin-off may improve the newly formed entity's visibility and market presence, which may improve its access to finance and present growth opportunities.

DowDuPont (DD)

The Dow Chemical Company and DuPont merged to establish DowDuPont Inc. in 2017. After the merger, DowDuPont was transformed into a multi-sector chemical giant with activities in agriculture, materials science, and specialized goods. The management of DD made the decision to divide the business into three distinct businesses, each focused on a different industry. The main goals were to increase the number of specialist enterprises, raise market awareness, and increase shareholder value.

Corteva (CTVA) was separated as a unique organization devoted to the agriculture industry in June 2019. Corteva concentrated on providing agricultural solutions, such as seeds, crop protection gear and electronic farming equipment. Corteva might narrow its attention to the difficulties and opportunities facing the agricultural sector by going independent. Several advantages resulted from Corteva's separation from DowDuPont, including better market visibility:

- **Specialization:** Corteva's spin-off gave it the ability to function as a specialized agriculture business, meeting just the requirements of farmers and agricultural clients. As a separate organization, Corteva could work on product development, innovation, and research specific to the agricultural industry.
- **Targeted marketing and communication:** As a standalone business, Corteva could focus on highlighting its knowledge and products in the agriculture industry. This focused strategy improved Corteva's market recognition and visibility.
- **Independent financial reporting:** As a result of Corteva's spin-off, it now has its own financial reporting, enabling investors to evaluate its results and prospects apart from those of the other DowDuPont firms.
- **Attractiveness to investors:** Investors now had the option of making direct investments in Corteva's agriculture-focused business, allowing them to match their investments with their unique interests and risk tolerance. The spin-off made investing more appealing to investors and enabled targeted investment choices. Post-spin-off, the increased market visibility, combined with its specialization, has helped Corteva gain recognition as a prominent player in the agriculture industry.

DD, CTVA, S&P 500 return, rebased to S&P, July 2019 to Jun 2023

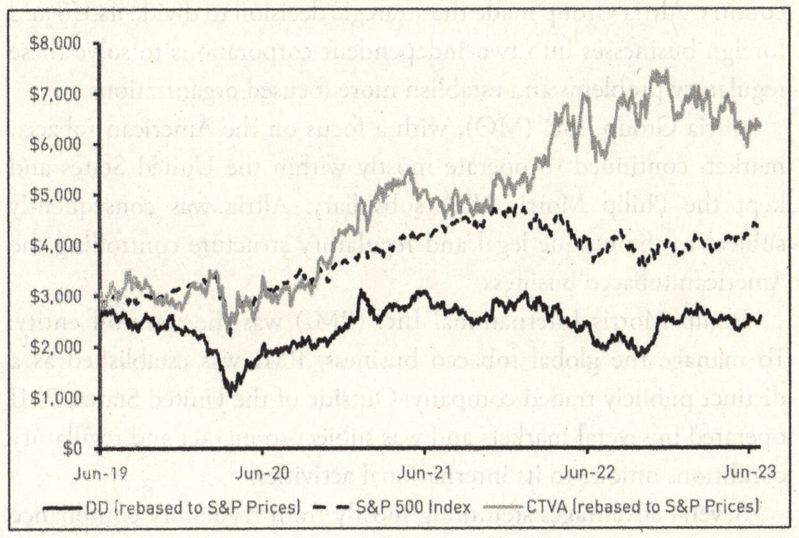

4. Regulatory compliance: To satisfy regulatory requirements or allay antitrust worries, some businesses may decide to spin off a business unit, especially if the combined entity's market dominance raises competition concerns.

Altria Group, Inc. (MO)

Altria Group, Inc. was a global tobacco and cigarette manufacturing company with a significant presence in the US. Its subsidiaries included Philip Morris, which focused on the US market, and Philip Morris International (PMI), which operated in international markets outside the United States.

The primary driver behind the spin-off was regulatory compliance related to the tobacco industry. The US has strict regulations on tobacco advertising, marketing and product packaging, as well as litigation risks associated with health-related lawsuits against tobacco companies. These regulations and litigations presented unique challenges and uncertainties for tobacco companies operating in the country. Altria Group made the strategic decision to divide its US and foreign businesses into two independent corporations to solve these regulatory problems and establish more focused organizations.

Altria Group, Inc. (MO), with a focus on the American tobacco market, continued to operate mostly within the United States and kept the Philip Morris USA subsidiary. Altria was consequently subject to the unique legal and regulatory structure controlling the American tobacco business.

Philip Morris International Inc. (PMI) was the spun-off entity: To manage the global tobacco business, PMI was established as a distinct publicly traded company. Outside of the United States, PMI operated in several markets and was subject to market and regulatory conditions unique to its international activities.

Several advantages stemming mostly from regulatory compliance were made possible by the split of Altria and PMI:

- **Focus on regulations:** The split allowed each business to concentrate on the regulations unique to its regional market. While PMI handled international regulatory environments, Altria could focus on dealing with laws and regulations in the United States.
- **Reduced litigation risks:** By keeping the US and international operations separate, each organization might handle its litigation risks and legal issues on its own, potentially reducing effects on the other company.
- **Clear market distinctions:** For investors and stakeholders, the spin-off established distinct markets. Separating Altria's concentration on the American tobacco market from PMI's global activities has made it easier for investors to evaluate the performance and prospects of the two companies.
- **Enhanced compliance mechanisms:** As distinct organizations, Altria and PMI could put in place compliance mechanisms specific to their markets, guaranteeing adherence to regional laws and industry standards.

MO, PM, S&P 500, rebased to S&P, March 2008 to May 2023

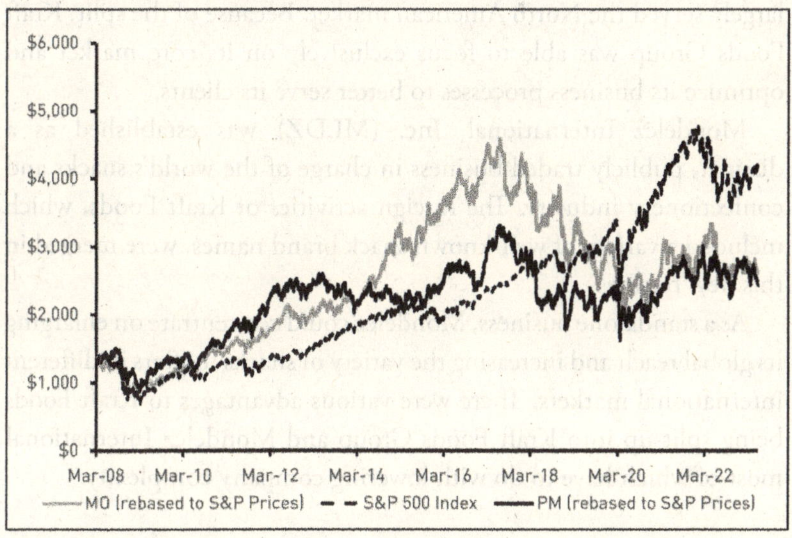

5. **Reduced company complexity:** A spin-off can streamline a company's structure and make it simpler for investors to evaluate and comprehend the firm if it operates in several unrelated industries.

Kraft Foods (KRFT)

Kraft Foods was a large global food and beverage corporation and operated in several markets, including those for cheese, snacks, beverages, and groceries. The organization's structure was complicated because of the company's wide range of brands and products.

The management of Kraft Foods realized that its inability to concentrate on its strategic priorities and core competencies was being hampered by the complexity of its business. The company made the decision to separate into two new entities, each with a focused business plan.

Kraft Foods Group, Inc. was established as a standalone entity devoted to its North American supermarket business. It continued to sell cheese, dairy, snack and supermarket brands, and products that largely served the North American market. Because of the split, Kraft Foods Group was able to focus exclusively on its core market and optimize its business processes to better serve its clients.

Mondelēz International, Inc. (MLDZ) was established as a distinct, publicly traded business in charge of the world's snacks and confectionery industry. The foreign activities of Kraft Foods, which included a variety of well-known snack brand names, were merged in this new business.

As a standalone business, Mondelēz could concentrate on enlarging its global reach and increasing the variety of snacks it offers in different international markets. There were various advantages to Kraft Foods being split up into Kraft Foods Group and Mondelēz International, most of which have to do with lowering company complexity:

- **Focused business strategies:** Each organization might match its resources, investment choices and business strategies to its market focus. While Mondelēz focused on the worldwide snacks market, Kraft Foods Group concentrated on the North American grocery market.
- **Operations made simpler:** By splitting into two businesses, Kraft Food's operations and organizational structure were made less complex. To maximize efficiency, organizations streamline supply chains, distribution systems and business operations.
- **Targeted resource allocation:** The spin-off enabled each business to devote resources more precisely to its core operations. Better capital allocation and investment choices were made as a result, which enhanced financial performance.
- **Investor clarity:** The spin-off gave investors a deeper knowledge of the financials, operations and development possibilities of each company. Investors were able to assess and compare the companies more effectively.

MDLZ, KRFT, S&P 500, rebased to S&P, October 2012 to March 2023

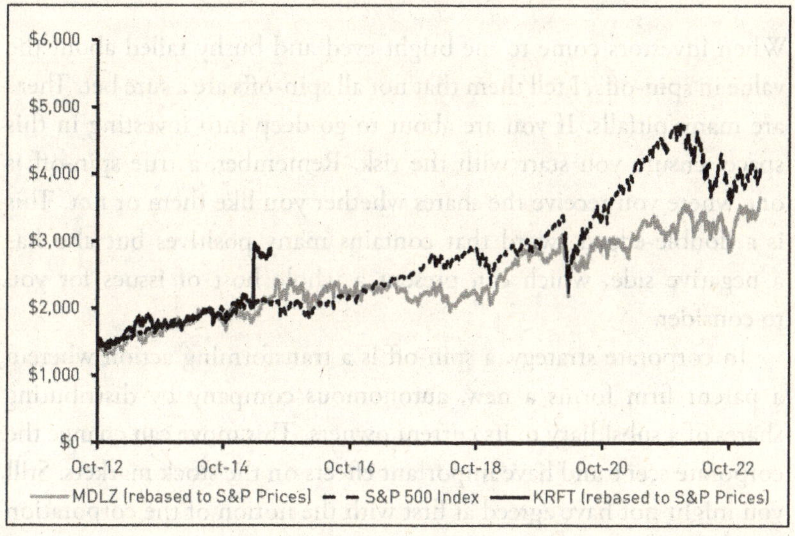

Companies can use the same corporate action for differing reasons:

- financial performance transparency and capital allocation efficiency
- to gain a competitive advantage, agility and flexibility
- better incentives for management
- easier strategic partnerships
- general business revitalization

It's crucial to remember that every company's choice to break up or undertake a spin-off is different and may combine a number of these primary factors. The strength of the businesses involved, the state of the market, and the efficient handling of the separation process are additional elements that affect a spin-off's success.

Possible Downsides of Spin-offs

When investors come to me bright eyed and bushy tailed about the value in spin-offs, I tell them that not all spin-offs are a sure bet. There are many pitfalls. If you are about to go deep into investing in this space, ensure you start with the risk. Remember, a true spin-off is one where you receive the shares whether you like them or not. This is a double-edged sword that contains many positives but also has a negative side, which can present a whole host of issues for you to consider.

In corporate strategy, a spin-off is a transforming action wherein a parent firm forms a new, autonomous company by distributing shares of a subsidiary to its current owners. This move can change the corporate scene and have important effects on the stock markets. Still, you might not have agreed at first with the notion of the corporation dissolving. You may thus find yourself with shares in a brand-new, foreign company you might not have wanted or know anything about. This can be very perplexing, particularly because it seems that every spin-off investment was previously a parent company stakeholder.

The company is typically a smaller, more focused industry player that has zero analyst coverage and has been dumped onto the market at no pre-determined price. Sometimes these are known as "orphan securities".

It's extremely important to look at the notifications from your broker about an impending spin-off in one of your holdings and try to understand the reasoning behind why the company is doing it. These transactions could release enormous value for your portfolio.

Important Events to Add to Your Calendar

Apart from valuation and trading strategy, which can be gained from your broker or trusted source and is a key step to carry out ahead of time, here are the three initial calendar points to look out for ahead of the transaction:

1. **Date of announcement and record:** The parent company makes the spin-off announcement and provides information about the new company's operations. A record date, or the day on which the parent company compiles the list of shareholders qualified to receive the spin-off shares, is also announced by the parent company.
2. **Proportionate allocation:** The parent company usually determines a proportionate distribution of spin-off shares to existing shareholders. This allocation is based on the number of shares held by each shareholder on the record date. For example, if the spin-off allocation ratio is 1:10, a shareholder with 100 shares in the parent company would receive ten shares of the new spun-off company.
3. **Trading day:** Spin-off shares can be traded on the exchange after they have been distributed, giving shareholders and investors the ability to buy and sell them on the open market.

Do Spin-offs Outperform?

I get this question all the time, and there is no single answer. On the whole, yes, but it isn't as easy as that – otherwise we could buy lots of them and watch the money roll in.

The spin-off process is often seen as an inefficient way of allocating shares because it doesn't necessarily target investors who are most interested in or suited for the new entity. In a spin-off, shares of the new company are distributed to existing shareholders of the parent company, regardless of their interest or desire for these new shares. As a result, many investors may end up with shares they didn't actively seek, and they might quickly sell them off in the market. This rapid selling can lead to the new company's stock being undervalued and overlooked by investors.

This situation creates a unique opportunity: the undervaluation and lack of initial interest can be a signal for savvy investors to investigate further, as it may reveal potential value that others are missing. This is the X that marks the spot where you should start digging.

Here is why spin-offs are an essential area for investors to analyze:

- Studies have shown that spin-offs have historically beaten the market by over 10% as the pure, newly focused business takes off.
- Compensation for executives can be more closely correlated with business performance. The company will become smaller, which will increase the executives' motivation and sense of ownership.
- Separating companies allows each entity to be properly valued and can sometimes unlock a "conglomerate discount".
- Due to the likelihood that the company would be small and lack a roadshow, it is under-followed. As a result, there are more chances for investors to discover returns greater than the index.
- The Edge's 20-year study shows that spin-offs are likely to be taken over. Roughly 35% are acquired at around the two-year mark post-spin-off.

Typically, there are hundreds of spin-off situations a year. Around 40 are over $1 billion market cap. This is a sweet spot, where liquidity and "real" companies come together.

Conclusion

For all the reasons given in this chapter, spin-offs are frequently seen as a reliable key to unlocking value. They can produce advantages for both the parent firm and the spun-off entity when they are carried out properly and thoughtfully, increasing value for shareholders.

However, it's crucial to remember that not all spin-offs will generate value, and there may be dangers and difficulties involved with the procedure. The quality of the underlying company, proper execution, market conditions, and the overall spin-off strategy all play a role in success. Identifying the reasons for the transaction is key, and that's where you start your analysis. Have I mentioned that before?

CHAPTER 6
How to Analyze and Invest in Spin-offs

- → Understanding Spin-off Dynamics
- → Evaluating the Spin-off Entity
- → Management and Leadership Assessment
- → Market Position and Competitive Analysis
- → Regulatory and Legal Considerations
- → Risks Assessment
- → Investment Valuation
- → Strategic Opportunities Post-Spin-off
- → Long-Term Prospects

Understanding Spin-off Dynamics

When a parent firm separates some of its assets, staff, and management to establish a new, independent company, a spin-off results, i.e. some of these resources are transferred to the new company. The creation of an independent company with its own legal standing, stock issuing, and management structure makes this separation essentially different from conventional investments or divestments.

Unique Features of Spin-offs

- Spin-offs become financially and operationally independent of their parent company. By means of this division, they can pursue their strategic goals, market prospects and innovation free from the limitations of the more general corporate structure.
- Without the deviations of the larger corporate agenda of the parent, the newly established firms can concentrate more precisely on their primary activities. More effective operations and quick adaptation to consumer needs or industry changes can result.
- Spin-offs' ability to uncover latent value usually helps them to get a good market acceptance. Investors may regard the parent and the new company more highly as distinct entities than as a merged company.

Strategic Argument for Spin-offs

Aiming to maximize corporate operations and improve shareholder value, companies spin off portions of their company for different strategic purposes. Important drivers for spin-offs include:

- Spin-offs have great capacity to unlock value for major shareholders. When buried inside a bigger firm, segments of a corporation that could be undervalued by the market can reach appropriate value as a concentrated, separate organization.
- Both the parent and the spin-off can focus better on their core skills, thereby optimizing processes and (ideally) raising profitability. This emphasis helps a business to invest in and grow its main areas free from the distraction of running a varied set of activities.
- Independent entities might draw investment more successfully. Companies with well-defined, targeted business strategies often pique the curiosity of investors more than conglomerates with several unrelated enterprises.
- Sometimes spin-offs are motivated by possible tax benefits that make the spin-off financially profitable, or by legal obligations to divestment of firm assets.

Investors thinking about this kind of investment must grasp the dynamics and strategic justification behind spin-offs. Because of their structural independence, strategic focus and ability to uncover value creation not usually obvious in conventional company configurations, spin-offs have special ingredients.

Examining the factors behind businesses' decisions to spin off divisions helps investors spot chances for value creation and expansion in the spin-off terrain. This information helps investors make wise selections consistent with their risk tolerance return profile.

Evaluating the Spin-off Entity

Investing in spin-offs calls for a sophisticated awareness both of their operational independence and their financial situation. This critical assessment reduces related risks while pointing out potentially lucrative investments.

Debt levels: You should examine the debt structure of the spin-off closely. For instance, Adient inherited a significant debt when it was spun off from Johnson Controls in 2016, which limited its financial freedom. Comparing the debt-to-equity ratio with industry norms helps one understand the financial soundness of the spin-off.

Revenue streams: One must first examine the spin-off's revenue stability. After its 2015 split from eBay, PayPal displayed good, rising income sources outside of its parent company, thereby demonstrating good market positioning and financial viability.

Profitability measures such as net margin and return on equity (ROE) provide an understanding of operational efficiency. For Ferrari, for example, looking at these numbers following its 2016 split from Fiat Chrysler would have shown a high-margin company, therefore highlighting its profitability.

Operational Independence: Key Factors to Consider

Management and governance: Good leadership is crucial. Zoetis from Pfizer in 2013 flourished under a management team that deftly guided the business into independence following a spin-off. Examining the management history and experience of the spin-off will help you have faith in its future performance.

Independence in operational systems, including IT and logistics, is essential. Mondelēz had to rapidly build its own worldwide operational infrastructure when Kraft Foods set off Mondelēz International in 2012; this was vital for the development of its worldwide market.

Strategic direction and resource allocation: It is key to know the strategic orientation of the spin-off. For instance, looking at how Conduent has been strategically realigning its business emphasis post-spin-off from Xerox in 2017 can help investors understand its long-term viability and how well the company uses its resources.

Examining the financial situation and operational independence of a spin-off using practical cases offers a strong basis for investment decisions. Investors are more suited to evaluate the possible hazards and benefits, guaranteeing a well-informed approach to including spin-offs into their portfolios.

Index Inclusion and Exclusion Dynamics of Spin-offs

Whether a spin-off is included in or removed from big market indices can significantly affect its stock's trajectory. Thanks to index fund automatic buying, inclusion usually results in better market visibility, investor interest and liquidity.

One prominent instance is when Zoetis was spun off from Pfizer and included on the S&P 500, greatly increasing its stock visibility and trading activity. Sophisticated investors should review the shareholder lists of parent companies within index funds. If a spin-off is deemed too small for index inclusion, investors can then calculate the potential volume of selling that might occur.

As of 28 March 2024, for inclusion in a major US index, companies must meet the following criteria:

- **Market capitalization:** Minimum of $15.78 billion, calculated by multiplying the share price with outstanding shares.
- **Liquidity:** High liquidity required, assessed using the float-adjusted liquidity ratio (FALR) – the annual dollar value traded divided by float-adjusted market capitalization (FMC).
- **Public float:** At least 10% of shares must be publicly available.

- **Earnings:** Positive earnings are required for the most recent quarter and cumulatively over the past four quarters.
- **Corporation type:** Eligible entities include corporations or real estate investment trusts (REITs) based in the US, excluding business development companies (BDCs), master limited partnerships (MLPs), limited liability companies (LLCs), closed-end funds (CEFs), and exchange-traded funds (ETFs).
- **Listing:** Must be listed on an eligible US exchange such as NYSE or NASDAQ.
- **Public company history:** Must have a public status for at least one year.

Management and Leadership Assessment

Understanding the viability and sustainability of a spin-off depends on evaluating its management quality and governance structure.

Experience and competence: Knowing the background for the management team is key. Take a spin-off, for instance: does the new CEO have a history of effective industry leadership – perhaps having guided similar businesses through phases of innovation and scale?

Stability of leadership: The presence of stable leaders is a sign of a clear, consistent strategic vision. For a big tech company, for example, a spin-off might gain by keeping leaders who have been essential in creating its main products.

Handling crises: The capacity of the leadership to control past crises can be a great indicator of their capacity to face upcoming difficulties. Their behavior during pivotal times, such as market declines or technology upheavals, reveals their strategic thinking and fortitude.

Government Structure

Examining corporate control: A strong board should include industry experts mixed with veterans with governance knowledge, therefore improving the quality of decisions made. Comprehensive control can be given by a varied board including people from many professional areas.

Transparency and responsibility: Good government is also typified by honest and continuous correspondence with stakeholders. Frequent and open reporting on operational difficulties, strategic projects and the financial situation guarantees responsibility and confidence among investors.

Compliance and ethics: Particularly in highly regulated sectors like pharmaceuticals and financial services, the spin-off's dedication to ethical behavior and regulatory norm compliance is vital. Strong compliance helps the business maintain its reputation and guards against legal problems.

A financial services spin-off creating a board with seasoned executives renowned for negotiating challenging regulatory environments and promoting ethical behavior, for example, is likely to inspire more investor confidence and market stability.

In essence, to predict a spin-off's operational performance and alignment with investor interests, you should evaluate its management and governance. Along with assessments of the quality and variety of the governance systems in place, investors should explore the industry experience, history of stability and effectiveness in former roles of the leadership.

Such an exhaustive study not only clarifies the preparedness of the spin-off to run independently but also helps to evaluate its resistance against obstacles. Key areas of interest for possible investors include effective leadership and governance, as they indicate the success of a spin-off in challenging markets.

Market Position and Competitive Analysis

Understanding the possible success of a spin-off in the market depends on analyzing its competitive strengths and market situation.

Analyzing the market: Analyze the extent and direction of growth of the market where the spin-off will function. For instance, given the growing need for artificial intelligence solutions across several sectors, the growth potential would be notable should a corporation such as IBM separate its Artificial Intelligence (AI) section.

Rivals: Name and evaluate the primary rivals. Think about how the spin-off stands in relation to market share, product range and technical capacity. If DuPont separates out a specialty chemicals division, for example, how does this division do against rivals such as BASF and Dow?

Trends in industry: Point up important developments that might affect the spin-off. Trends in a healthcare spin-off can be toward personalized treatment or more healthcare digitization, which would create fresh prospects.

Finding Special Competent Edges

Technological superiority: Does the spin-off have an edge from owned technologies? For instance, NVIDIA's advanced AI and deep learning powers would help a spin-off focused in autonomous driving technologies.

Operating procedures: Evaluate whether the spin-off boasts better operating procedures than its rivals. Using Amazon's very effective supply chain and distribution capabilities, a spin-off concentrating on logistics solutions may outperform rivals like FedEx and UPS.

Brand power: Strong brand recognition and a dedicated client base would help a corporation like Coca-Cola prosper should it separate a fast-growing beverage line from its parent company.

Strategic alliances: Review alliances meant to improve the position of the company. For example, there may be a major competitive advantage if a renewable energy division spun out from General Electric finds a battery storage solution in cooperation with Tesla.

Evaluating the potential of the spin-off depends on careful examination of its market position and competitive advantages. This should consider technology assets, operational efficiencies, brand power, and strategic alliances, which taken together offer a comprehensive picture of the competitive scene and future possibilities of the spin-off.

Regulatory and Legal Considerations

Examining spin-offs calls for careful assessment of the legal and regulatory environments that can affect their operations and financial situation. Compliance rules are priority; the spin-off has to negotiate a complicated web of industry-specific rules that might greatly affect its profitability and business operations. If a pharmaceutical company separates a biotech business, for example, the new company must follow strict FDA rules about drug approvals and clinical studies, which can be expensive and time-consuming.

You should give great weight to legal risks. Many times, spin-offs inherit responsibilities from their parent corporations that could cause major legal difficulties down the road. For instance, if a manufacturing corporation separates a unit formerly engaged in operations with environmental hazards, the new entity may inherit any obligations linked to environmental clean-up and litigation. This was evident when DuPont set out Chemours, which subsequently drew significant environmental claims stemming from DuPont's prior activities.

Spin-offs also must create their own legal frameworks and contracts, which could entail renegotiating or creating fresh supplier agreements, customer agreements and employee contracts. The capacity of these legal systems to let the spin-off run free without encountering legal issues will be much influenced by their fit.

Investors should also consider the spin-off's capacity to follow foreign laws should it operate in multiple countries. This includes adherence to cross-border trade rules, tax laws and international business practices, all of which vary greatly depending on the country and affect the company's worldwide operations.

To grasp the sustainability and durability of a spin-off, you must first thoroughly assess the regulatory compliance criteria and possible legal hazards. Investors should be aware of the inherited liabilities and the sufficiency of the legal structure of the spin-off to manage such obstacles. Knowing these factors helps you to evaluate if the spin-off has the required legal and regulatory systems in place to flourish as an independent business, and to understand the legal obstacles it might face in the future.

Financial Risks: Knowing Financial Exposures

Examining spin-offs requires you to consider operational as well as financial issues that might compromise the stability and expansion possibilities of the new company.

Market volatility: Particularly vulnerable to this is spin-off activity, especially that of recently independent companies. Until the market fully appreciates the new company model and its prospects, their performance could be more erratic. For instance, the initial reaction of the market might greatly affect the stock price of a technological company that separates a fast-expanding but non-profit segment.

Post-spin-off changes to the capital structure are typical as the new company tries to create a financial basis fit for its operations and expansion plans. This could call for increasing fresh debt or equity, therefore influencing the leverage and financial freedom of the business. For example, a heavy industrial spin-off taking on significant debt to support additional activities may have more financial strain, especially if market circumstances worsen.

Operating risks: Establishing independent systems that were formerly under the control of the parent company poses one of the main operational hazards. This covers consumer interactions, logistics, human resources, and IT systems. For daily operations, the efficiency of these systems is vital. The inaccurate setup of these systems could cause operational disturbances and higher expenses.

Spin-offs must define their operational procedures, which can call for hiring fresh staff, renegotiating new vendor contracts, and creating new manufacturing or service delivery standards. These developments can bring hazards pertaining to operational breakdowns or delays. For example, if a consumer products firm separates its beverage division, the new company will have to build its supply chain and distribution systems quickly to guarantee product availability and preserve customer contentment.

Investors examining spin-offs should carefully consider operational as well as financial concerns. Financial exposures connected to changes in capital structure and market volatility call for rigorous study to ascertain how they might affect the financial situation of the spin-off.

Likewise, the capacity of the new organization to operate freely and compete successfully depends on operational risks related to establishing new systems and reaching operational readiness. Understanding these risks helps investors evaluate the potential difficulties and possibilities for the spin-off, thus guiding wise investment selections.

Investment Valuation

Making wise judgments, for investors thinking about spin-offs, depends on knowing valuation measures and ideal investing timing. Fair value of a spin-off is mostly determined by widely used methodologies such as the discounted cash flow (DCF) analysis or similar company analysis. Using DCF, for example, calls for forecasts of future cash flows, which might be difficult for a young company but provides an overall picture of its valuation depending on predicted performance.

Also valuable are ratios including enterprise-value-to-EBITDA (EV/EBITDA), price-to-earnings (P/E), and price-to-sales (P/S). These ratios provide information on whether the spin-off is overpriced or undervalued, enabling a comparison between it and its industry peers. Analyzing a media business's digital assets using these ratios versus digital media rivals, for instance, helps you to better understand valuation if the company separates these assets.

Timing of Investments: Examining Entry and Exit Points

You must first understand the current dynamics of the market. Entering during a market slump, for instance, might let investors buy shares at a reduced price provided the spin-off has good foundations.

The timing of the spin-off depends also on its stage of life. Initially volatile newly spun-off enterprises may provide risk-tolerant investors with purchase prospects. On the other hand, leaving could be best when the spin-off enters a mature stage, especially if development slows and the market begins to value it more conservatively.

Specific events over the lifetime of a spin-off, such as the introduction of new projects or fulfillment of important milestones, might generate ideal investment windows. Investing immediately after a successful product release by the spin-off, for example, might leverage good market momentum.

Analyzing spin-offs requires a thorough evaluation of valuation criteria to ascertain their fair market value and strategic study of the ideal moments to enter or leave the venture. By means of financial models and knowledge of market conditions in relation to the lifetime of the spin-off, investors can maximize rewards while controlling risk.

Combining these analytical components helps investors create a more focused strategy for investing in spin-offs, one that will match financial commitments to the most exciting stages of spin-off development.

Strategic Opportunities Post-Spin-off

In evaluating the prospects and investment possibilities of spin-offs, you should get to know their growth plans and possible acquisition dynamics. Spin-offs frequently have more flexibility than their parent company to enter new markets. This could call for geographical development or diversification into other product categories. If a consumer electronics division is spun out from a bigger corporation, for example, it might innovate with new smart technology goods or pursue unexplored markets in underdeveloped nations.

Product or service innovation is a major engine of spin-off growth. This could entail improving already-existing items or creating fresh technology to satisfy changing consumer demand. Aiming to produce innovative treatments, a spin-off from a pharmaceutical business, for example, can heavily invest in biotechnology developments.

Potential Buyers: Identifying Targets for Acquisitions

Larger firms seeking to improve their skills or market position may find spin-offs – especially those in high-growth sectors – to be attractive targets. Strategic buyers find great value in the spin-off because of its scalability and specialty.

Spin-offs could instead seek expansion by means of acquisitions, thereby contrasting from each other. This approach can rapidly scale their activities, increase their market share or improve their technological capability. To include advanced AI features into its current products, a recently independent tech business might, for example, buy smaller startups.

Analyzing the development plans and possible spin-off acquisitions helps you to fully appreciate their appeal as an investment and expansion possibility. Investors can estimate the possibility of notable development and market influence by looking at how spin-offs intend to penetrate new markets, innovate, or engage in acquisition operations. The long-term value and performance of spin-offs in competitive sectors depend on these elements rather significantly. Combining these ideas will help investors make better selections in line with spin-offs with strong development paths and strategic acquisition ambitions.

Long-Term Prospects

Evaluating the long-term survival and possible future achievements of spin-offs requires a thorough investigation of their stand-alone possibilities as well as the larger industry dynamics that might affect their performance.

Operating with a sustainable business plan will help a spin-off be successful over the long run. This covers a strong financial situation, a competitive product or service range, and a clear strategic direction. For instance, the success of a major technological company separating its cloud computing branch would mostly rely on its capacity to innovate and control expenses in a very competitive industry.

A spin-off will be defined by its capacity to adjust to technological developments and changes in the market. This includes reacting to consumer needs, legislative changes and technological upheavals. A spin-off that constantly develops its products and business plans is more likely to be successful in the long term.

Industry Patterns Affect Future Performance

Sector-specific dynamics: You should be aware of the developments in the industry from which the spin-off starts. For example, a telemedicine-focused healthcare spin-off will gain from the growing trend of digital health services, hence promoting its long-term development.

Technological innovations: The speed of invention in fields including technology and biotechnology can greatly affect the performance of a spin-off. Investing in R&D and keeping ahead of technical curves will help a spin-off use fresh developments to get a competitive edge.

Economic and regulatory factors: Depending on their sector, changes in regulations and economic fluctuations could also affect spin-offs differently. Environmental laws, for instance, may impact spin-offs in the energy industry and force them to make investments in greener technologies or risk losing market relevance.

A spin-off's long-term prospects depends on its capacity to keep viable business operations and adjust to macro- and microeconomic changes. Investors can estimate the future success of spin-off investments by means of analysis of sustainable business practices, flexibility and industry trend influence.

This thorough knowledge enables investors to make wise judgments in line with spin-offs showing potential not only in present circumstances but also in their capacity to flourish in the future environment molded by continuous industry developments and advances.

CHAPTER 7

Capitalizing on Management and Insider Transactions

- What Investors do Wrong?
- Where to Find and Analyze Insider Transactions
- Types of Insiders and Who to Follow
- Management Analysis

TO MAKE GAINS and be ahead of the masses in the stock market, I frequently say, look in places that others aren't. Smart investing is about not only this, but also looking in the right places. It's not about being first, contrary to popular belief. The rub? You usually have to do a little more work, and that doesn't fit well with most investors who are after a quick profit.

Monitoring company executives buying and selling their own shares is an absolute must for our firm and clients, and an essential ingredient to analyze when approaching an investment. I mean, why wouldn't you want to buy and sell with the people who know what's going on in their company? Of course you would, but the interpretation and mimicking of their stock transactions can leave you with big losses if you fail to do the analysis and just blindly do what they do. Let's clarify the concept of trading by company executives in their own shares, because it's not always obvious.

Illegal Insider Trading

Insider trading involves the trading in the stock of a publicly traded firm by a person who, for any reason, possesses non-public, material knowledge (information) about that stock. Depending on the time the insider makes the trade, insider trading can be either legal or illegal.

What exactly is material information? It has no clear meaning, but it might be broadly interpreted as any information relevant to a company that a stockholder considering buying or selling would deem significant enough to take into account before making the trade.

The US Securities and Exchange Commission (SEC) is very active in tracking illegal transactions by using market surveillance tools and general whistleblowers, so this comes with a warning: don't try this at home. Having said that, the rise of the derivatives market has made it extremely difficult for the SEC to identify the misuse of privileged information. Buying stock can be hugely leveraged with options, but because of their nature, I'd advise that you seek financial guidance before using them to supplement your stock trades.

Martha Stewart is an American businesswoman, writer and TV personality – and also a convicted felon. She is a media icon who built a business empire throughout the 1990s and 2000s with the TV show she hosted, *Martha Stewart Living*, with each episode presenting insights on things such as cooking, gardening, arts and crafts, and decorating. She was extremely successful in the time of high consumerism and had America at her feet, but things went horribly wrong.

Sam Waksal, the CEO of ImClone and a friend of Stewart's, learned that the FDA had not yet approved the company's promising experimental cancer medication. Before the news, which was certain to send the price of ImClone stock tumbling, Waksal attempted to sell his shares. As soon as she received word from Peter Bacanovic, the Merrill Lynch broker she shared with the Waksal family, Martha Stewart liquidated all of her own shares in ImClone for around $230,000. Both transactions were carried out ahead of the public knowing, and it was deemed to be insider trading.

The SEC claims that Stewart avoided a $45,673 loss by selling all 3928 shares of her ImClone Systems stock on 27 December 2001, after obtaining this important, secret information from Bacanovic. Her selling resulted in a 16% decline in the stock value the next day.

Stewart was found guilty in March 2004 of the felonies of obstruction of an agency proceeding, conspiracy to obstruct and making false statements to federal investigators following a highly publicized six-week jury trial. In July 2004, she was given a five-month sentence to serve in a federal prison.

Stewart's case is just one of many high-profile illegal insider trading cases over the years, though they are not that common. More recently, in 2011, Raj Rajaratnam, CEO of the Galleon Group hedge fund, was sentenced to 11 years in prison. He was involved in the insider trading of more than 15 companies. He also paid a penalty of nearly $93 million. The SEC also alleged that Rajaratnam orchestrated a large insider trading ring. The trial included former McKinsey CEO and Goldman board member Rajat Gupta.

In November 2013, the giant hedge fund SAC Capital, founded by Steve Cohen, agreed to a $1.8 billion fine for insider trading. That involved the stocks of more than 20 companies from 1999 to 2000. It was alleged that Cohen's lawyer negotiated the huge fine to avoid jail time.

He was previously charging some of the highest fees in the industry with his fund. Wikipedia says he charged a 3% management fee and 50% performance fee over the same period – nice work if you can get it! It certainly made him very rich. As of September 2024, Steve Cohen's net worth is estimated to be around $22 billion.

Many years ago, I stood in front of a very traditional group of fund managers in northern England. I was going through the way I looked at companies and how I approached an investment. The presentation was going well, and as I flipped to the next slide I announced, "The next area which you should be looking at to make a return on is insider trading." The room erupted with laughter. In hindsight, I probably could have phrased things a little differently.

Insider trading was much more of an issue in the 1990s, as the authorities were still coming to grips with how to track it. Investors were confused and weary. It was and still is viewed as a highly criminal activity, and there I was standing in front of a crowd of people with a fiduciary responsibility handling other people's money telling them to break the law (or so it seemed). Nothing could have been further from the truth.

I went on to explain the legal side of insider trading and following the people who matter into their investments by their trading actions. SEC Rule 10b-5 forbids corporate officers, directors and other insider staff from utilizing proprietary information to gain an advantage (or protect against a disadvantage) while trading in the company's stock. The "tipping" of proprietary corporate information to outside parties is likewise prohibited under this guideline.

Legal Insider Trading

When corporate insiders such as officers, directors, employees, and significant shareholders purchase and sell stock in their own firms and inform the authorities, this is legal insider trading. Insiders of corporations are required to notify the SEC when they trade their own securities. There may be a delay before insider data reporting reaches the typical investor. The SEC requires Form 4 filings to be completed when there are ownership changes within two business days of a trade.

Sales of stock are a little more contentious when it comes to the insiders. When an insider wishes to sell restricted, unregistered or controlled securities, they must submit a Form 144 to the SEC. Prior to the sale, an insider must file this form on paper with the SEC. A Form 144 covers the insider's sales for the following three months.

In essence, executives are filing these forms just after they have traded, and you as an investor can monitor them and decide if you want to follow them. Easy, yeah? Not so fast. The main problem that I frequently see with investors, individuals and the media is not the monitoring process of the transactions, but the interpretation of them. Overall, they generally take what they see and fail to dig any deeper.

Here at The Edge, we track and analyze all the insiders' trading activity to determine specific patterns coupled with our fundamental analysis to work out which of the insiders are the ones who matter. You might find this odd, but not all insiders are good at buying their own company stock. Remember this.

You must first figure out what the transaction is about. It could be one of three things:

- **A 10b5-1 plan:** Insiders can make trading plans ahead of time if they choose a date or price at which to execute a transaction thanks to the 10b5-1 judgment (either a purchase or a sale). The trade is initiated after the event has taken place. The 10b5-1 plans are used for these trades. Being pre-planned, they have little significance to future share price moves.

- **Stock options:** This is a complete red herring for future stock direction purposes. These "trades" are essentially free money in the form of stock that has been given to the executives, usually at a discount. They gain it virtually as a free giveaway and sell it at a profit. It really has no implications on stock direction but does have significance when you are analyzing incentives. The media in particular frequently make incorrect assumptions here.
- **Buys and sells:** When executives put their hands in their pockets and buy stock using their own money, this is one of the most powerful signals you will see, but again, more analysis is needed. One of the greatest investors of all time, Peter Lynch, was noted as saying that "insiders might sell their shares for any number of reasons, but they buy them for only one: they think the price will rise." He's correct of course, but this is where you start your analysis.

So, you've established a framework for monitoring trades and you've worked out what to look for. Now you need to analyze how significant the purchase really is. Here at The Edge, we rely on many years of data to identify not only the pattern of historical transactions, but the key insiders who are good at buying their own stock. It's in fact very rare for executives to sell their own shares and the company to come out with bad news, because, as we have seen, they end up in jail. On the whole, then, I'd ignore the sales unless it's the one exception where the executive is selling into price weakness, which indicates the share (company) is weak and has potentially further to fall. This initially is a huge red flag.

There are several other areas where we analyze the purchases of executives. These include the dollar amount bought or sold, the amount in relation to how much they own already, their net worth, and whether historically they have been value buyers (they are buying because they believe their company is cheap) or catalyst buyers ahead of an event. One thing remains: purchases only count if they are in the open market.

My good friend and long-term market professional George Muzea has written an excellent book on insiders. George has been around over 40 years and has worked with the likes of George Soros and Stanley Druckenmiller and is the world expert on insiders and their behavior. I lean on him for his valuable advice all the time. He's also a super nice guy.

George says that the biggest mistake he sees with investors is buying with every insider buy that comes along via the Bloomberg terminal or as reported in the media without doing any kind of analysis of the insider's record or seeing if it's value buying or catalytic buying. He clarifies, "80% of all insiders are value buyers. They buy when their stocks drop to or below book value or their perception of intrinsic value. In bear markets you ignore them and wait for the stocks to bottom out and when the stock starts an uptrend and they buy again, then we buy as well. This group of buyers are called catalytic insider buyers as they know good news is coming."

Company executives sell for a variety of reasons. Most people, including company executives, are not awash with cash these days. They are invested in their own company (me for one), in other entities, or in other financial vehicles. Consequently, when a need for cash arrives, something usually must be liquidated. This need could take the form of a new boat, a new house, college tuition fees, health issues, or even a divorce. There is usually not a reason attached when an insider sells. Everyone works for a salary but also needs liquidity when these events come up.

Think of another scenario: you join a company and get discounted stock options. The stock then moves higher, and you want to realize some of that new wealth, so you sell some stock. The run-of-the-mill employee wouldn't think about valuation.

There is a situation where it is important to watch when a director sells, but we will come to that later. It comes down to the fact that you will be very unlucky if your directors sell, and bad news comes out. It will also be *very* unlucky for them, but it's possible. However, just like fraud, there's no way to really know.

Now let's look at the other side. The side you should be interested in and which contains a catalyst. What should you be looking at? Remember this one thing:

Insiders Buy For One Reason Only

So, what should you look for when you are considering looking for ideas using insider trading analysis? The expectation is that the stock is going to rise.

Here are three areas you should be looking at:

1. **Who else has knowledge about company accounts?:** CEOs, CFOs and company secretaries are all boardroom executives you should be watching. However, it's not enough that these people are buying. You need to examine how much they held previously, what percentage they're buying in relation to what they hold, what their net worth is and, most importantly for me, you should be establishing whether they are value buyers (buying because the stock is cheap) or catalyst buyers (previous history of buying on events). Examine the incentives for the management. How do they get paid with the stock price? We will look at this key area here.
2. **Watch the non-executive directors:** This is a little bit of gold that you won't hear mentioned in many places, if at all. Non-executive directors are not involved in the day-to-day running of the company. They sit on the board, watch, listen and add their input; however, they are not really involved in the operations. Consequently, they have a different view of the company and have a better understanding of the environment in which the company operates, and of the valuation of the company shares, as they can look from afar and better analyze the environment.
3. **Only open-market purchases count:** As mentioned, executives using their own cash to buy shares in their company is a powerful signal. Stock options given to executives don't really count. Also, watch cluster buying: two, three or four executives, whether they are non-executive or not, is a key indicator that something may be about to happen. Watch the filings carefully. It will complement your fundamental analysis very well.

For a long time, I thought that selling by insiders didn't matter. After all, directors sell for a variety of reasons. However, when an insider sells stock on the open market, the media, press and most investors typically just look at the trade and ignore the characteristics.

How often have you read a headline that runs something like, "Directors Sell XXX Number of Shares at XXX Price"? Most investors will be put off the stock immediately. There is something about company insiders selling that appears negative. Why should you invest in something that the very people who run the company are bailing out of? There are occasions where insider selling is important, and we outline this in our chapter on shorts.

Value Buyers and Catalyst Buyers

As mentioned, there are two types of insider buyers: value buyers and catalyst buyers. Value buyers, as the name suggests, are buyers of cheap levels on their own stock. They recognize value when they see it and they know what their stock is worth. They buy when it's cheap and they sell when it's expensive. Watching out for these guys will add to your conviction when buying the stock.

Then there are the catalyst buyers. Arguably, these are much more important. They make up about 20% of the insider buying. As suggested, they buy ahead of an announcement or event. They should be watched. A few things you should look at carefully with insiders:

1. **How much stock do they currently own?** They should be well invested into their own company.
2. **What historical compensation and incentives have they been given?** Aligning incentives with corporate outlook objectives is a good clue as to whether the executive responds to incentivization and therefore has the share price at heart.
3. **What is their history?** How good have they been in the past at buying their own shares? Not all directors are good at buying their own stock.

Insider buying is a great hunting ground for investments because analysts overlook it. They shouldn't. I always check if there has been any insider activity on any of my investments and you should too. But don't let this stop you from starting with the insiders. Remember, insiders tend to have a six-month view of a company.

One last thing to note and have in your armory. It doesn't always happen, but you should also look for directors buying into strength and selling into weakness. These can be some of the best signals you ever get. On the buying side, it's either a real conviction that the company is headed the right way or, on the sale side, the wrong way. A company executive selling into weakness of his company share price is the only sale I would take note of and conduct more investigation.

Case Study: Pfizer Inc. (PFE)

The greatest pandemic of modern times hit the world in early 2020 and started to gain traction throughout the rest of the year. There was no cure and governments were coming to terms with something they had never experienced before.

But what was interesting in the same year was that Pfizer (PFE), a major American pharmaceutical company, was looking to spin off its Upjohn unit, which immediately would be merged with Mylan to form Viatris, effective 16 November 2020, in a transaction tax-free to Pfizer shareholders. Viatris aside, this would make PFE a much cleaner business post-spin.

PFE (Parent ex-Spin-merger) would position itself as a focused innovative biopharma company, with a superior revenue growth profile of 6% (compared to the industry's 4%) and a double-digit (10%+) bottom-line growth for the next five years (from FY21 to FY25E).

In 1H2020 alone, PFE registered 9% operational revenue growth, and there would be no significant loss of patents for PFE in sight through 2026. So, the fundamentals were looking good pre-spin. They were also at the forefront in finding a vaccination.

The Key Insiders Were Buying

A closer look at what was going on behind the scenes seemed to back up the quality financial outlook. Wall Street deal maker Ronald E. Blaylock had just made his first investment in Pfizer stock three years after he joined the board – signaling there was about to be an upward move in the company's fortunes.

The Corporate Governance insider, who sits on the Audit Committee, snapped up $500k shares just three weeks ago, ahead of the hotly anticipated Q4 $195 billion Mylan (MYL) and Upjohn Spin-off (Viatris).

A Pfizer director since 2017, Mr Blaylock, 60, founded top US investment banking firm Blaylock & Company, later the private equity firm GenNx360, and originally served on Pfizer's Science and Technology Committee.

Renowned for his banking skills and philanthropy, Blaylock advised on over $150 billion worth of transactions in 2005. He was named one of the Most Powerful Blacks on Wall Street by Black Enterprise Magazine and has sat on the Board of Trustees of Carnegie Hall, NYU, the Inner-City Scholarship Fund, and on Prep for Prep, which helps gifted children attain scholarships to attend private schools.

Coincidentally, the only other Pfizer insider to have bought shares in the past nine years also served on Pfizer's Science and Technology Committee. Former FDA Commissioner Dr Scott Gottlieb, 48, is a Special Partner with venture capital firm New Enterprise Associates (NEA), and is a shrewd operator, like Mr Blaylock. When he joined the Pfizer board the previous year, Dr Gottlieb spent $104,160 buying 3000 shares, and in January 2020 he bought a further 1000 shares, spending $37,000, giving a very positive indication that change was afoot.

No other insiders have bought Pfizer shares since 2011, so these purchases ahead of a corporate change in the company and the wider landscape changing caused us to sound the alarm bells. Not simply because of Pfizer's attempts to have a coronavirus vaccine in circulation by October, which could see the share price rocket (giving investors huge returns), but also because Pfizer has a sensational track record in spin-offs. Take Zoetis (ZTS), the world's largest producer of medicine and vaccinations for animals, which was spun in 2013. Investors have had stellar returns, with +289% yields, beating the S&P's +16% return in the same period.

As part of Operation Warp Speed, the US government had a goal to begin delivering 300 million doses of a vaccine for Covid-19 in 2021. They had placed an initial order with Pfizer and its partner BioNTech of 100 million doses for $1.95 billion following FDA authorization or approval, and could acquire up to 500 million additional doses. Americans would receive the vaccine for free, consistent with the US government's commitment for free access for Covid-19 vaccines.

"We've been committed to making the impossible possible by working tirelessly to develop and produce in record time a safe and effective vaccine to help bring an end to this global health crisis," said Dr Albert Bourla, Pfizer Chairman and CEO. "We made the early decision to begin clinical work and large-scale manufacturing at our own risk to ensure that product would be available immediately if our clinical trials prove successful and an Emergency Use Authorization is granted. We are honored to be a part of this effort to provide Americans access to protection from this deadly virus."

"Expanding Operation Warp Speed's diverse portfolio by adding a vaccine from Pfizer and BioNTech increases the odds that we will have a safe, effective vaccine as soon as the end of this year," said US Department of Health and Human Services Secretary Alex Azar. "Depending on success in clinical trials, today's agreement will enable the delivery of approximately 100 million doses of this vaccine to the American people."

With news that the Trump administration was considering fast-tracking an experimental coronavirus vaccine from the UK for use in America ahead of the presidential election, the race began to heat up. As stated in an August 2020 article in the *Financial Times*, the US Food and Drug Administration was considering awarding "emergency use authorization" (EUA) in October 2020 to a vaccine then being developed in a partnership between AstraZeneca and Oxford University. This opened the door to Pfizer, which was also trialing vaccines and planning to enroll 30,000 participants in Phase III studies they started in July of that year.

And so, with good fundamental numbers supporting the company, a corporate catalyst event ahead and heavy buying by key insiders, we advised clients to start buying the shares in August 2020. The stock went sideways for a while and then, with the pandemic becoming deeper and with PFE ahead of the game with vaccinations, the share price rocketed from $36.41 on 25 August 2020 to a high a little more than a year later, on 16 December 2021, of $61.25. That's a 68% gain. The S&P index was higher by 36% over the same period. The insiders knew what was coming and they capitalized on it.

PFE, volume, S&P 500, rebased to PFE, August 2020 to October 2022

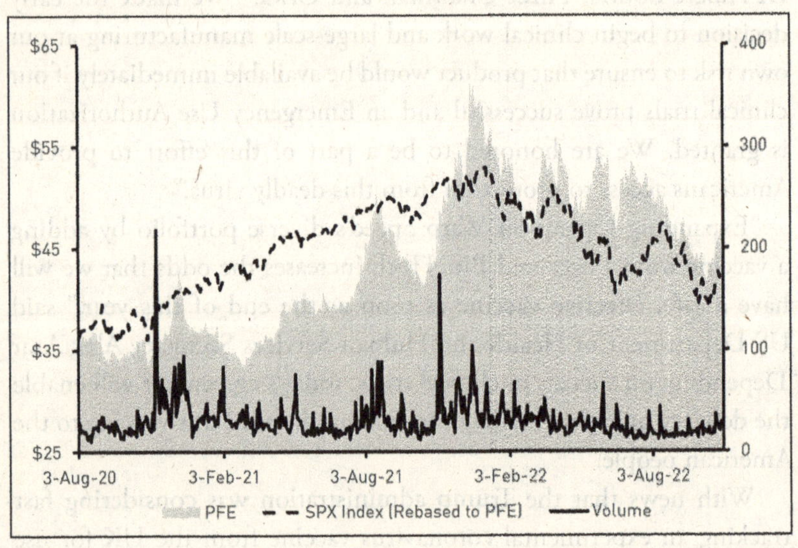

CHAPTER 8

The Rationale Behind Special Situations

- → Types Of Special Situation
- → Why Do They Matter?
- → Special Situations
- → Mergers & Acquisitions
- → Spin-offs
- → Bankruptcies & Restructurings
- → Rights Offerings
- → The Proxy Contest

THE PURPOSE OF stock special situations is to capitalize on opportunities unique to the stock market that arise because of events or circumstances. These circumstances typically involve occurrences that can cause a substantial change in a company's stock price. The goal of special situations is to find market inefficiencies caused by unexpected events or circumstances and capitalize on them. To appropriately weigh the risks and benefits in unusual circumstances, in-depth investigation and analysis are typically required. By capitalizing on these one-of-a-kind openings in the stock market, investors who focus on these methods hope to produce above-average profits.

These situations can result from both internal and external factors, and their underlying causes vary widely.

It's crucial to screen for specific keywords, as they can reveal opportunities that often go unnoticed by the mainstream, allowing you to investigate and analyze potential investments that others might miss.

These opportunities can be driven by mispricing, market inefficiencies or shifts in investor sentiment. Remember, finding these "special situations" requires work, so if you're not prepared to do the work, stop reading now. I asked the legendary investor Joel Greenblatt once on our company webinar, "If special situations and spin-offs are so lucrative, why isn't everyone doing them?" Straight of the bat he replied, "Because investors don't want to do the work." He's right of course. If you want to outperform, do the work.

There are three reasons to look at these anomalies within companies in the market:

1. Special situations can present an opportunity for investors to profit from companies trading at a discount to their intrinsic worth, so there is the possibility of a very high return in some cases.
2. Some situations carry inherent risk, but investors can mitigate that risk by selecting companies with solid fundamentals.
3. Unique situations can introduce investors to under-the-radar companies that are under-reported on by Wall Street pros and the media.

Hard and Soft Catalysts

Special situations fall into two categories: hard and soft catalysts. Soft catalysts are events or news that are likely to have a positive impact on a company's stock price, but the impact is difficult to quantify. Hard catalysts are events or news that are likely to have a significant and immediate impact on a company's stock price. Personally, I prefer hard catalysts to soft ones, because they are quantifiable.

Earnings reports, management changes, new product launches, industry trends, sentiment and share buybacks are all examples of soft catalysts. They can impact the stock price over time.

Hard catalysts can include mergers and acquisitions, legal and regulatory events, spin-offs, split-offs, Reverse Morris Trusts or involvement from an activist investor.

A hard catalyst, such as an announced merger, tends to have a defined outcome, which creates a more predictable return. A soft catalyst, perhaps a company undergoing a senior management change, can have a range of outcomes.

Why Do They Matter?

This is where it gets interesting. I am a big fan of ensuring that there is some sort of catalyst with my investing. I've seen so many value investors buy stocks because they are "cheap", but as we know, some companies will stay cheap forever.

You must have an appreciation for catalysts. Investors can evaluate and reduce the risks connected with their investments by first recognizing the events that could have an impact on a stock. This is of paramount importance for preventing losses and keeping capital intact. Moreover, triggers typically determine when investments are made. Based on their estimates of how catalysts may play out, investors may decide to purchase, hold or sell equities. Investment results can be greatly affected by timing, and for that reason it's important to keep up with catalyst developments.

Understanding the significance of numerous triggers becomes even more important when applied to diversified portfolios. To maximize their portfolios, investors need to strike a balance in regards to their exposure to diverse catalyst-driven events, as different equities may have different reactions to the same catalyst. Your capital allocation choices will also be affected by catalysts. To mitigate risk, investors may prefer sectors or equities that are less likely to be affected by unfavorable catalysts. The influence on returns can be substantial when capital is allocated strategically. Catalysts can affect the long-term success of a business, not just its immediate performance. Long-term investors need to be aware of how catalysts affect the underlying strengths and market standing of a company.

In addition, catalysts typically result in elevated market volatility, providing chances for traders seeking rapid profits at the expense of longer-term investors. Traders can profit from price fluctuations if they have a firm grasp of the factors that cause them. Catalysts affect market sentiment in ways other than price changes. Optimism and investor confidence might rise in response to a positive catalyst, whereas negative ones can cause anxiety and nervousness. Trading patterns and stock prices are subsequently influenced by market mood. Catalysts also play a role in the very important process of due diligence, which is part of each investment. Catalysts are considered by investors throughout the due diligence process. They evaluate the potential effects of external factors on the company's bottom line, market share and future growth.

Finally, triggers often elicit fear and greed in investors, respectively driving purchases and sales. You can better retain discipline and make logical decisions despite market swings if you have a firm grasp of how investor psychology interacts with catalysts.

Special Situations: Mergers and Acquisitions

Whenever I mention the words "special situations" to investors, they always think of mergers and acquisitions (M&A). These situations can provide value, but personally they are not the first event I look for. To be honest, M&A should be left to the professional investor. However, if you decide to go down this path, start with the risks first. You should remember there are significant risks, but also substantial profits assuming the deal goes through smoothly. The three main risks of M&A are:

Deal failure risk: The largest risk is the end of a trade. However, not every planned merger or acquisition materializes. Regulatory hurdles, finance problems and shareholder unhappiness are just some of the reasons deals fall through. Therefore, arbitrageurs who paid a premium for the target company's stock may witness a decline in the value of their investment.

Regulatory and antitrust risk: If government agencies have reason to believe that a merger or acquisition may result in anticompetitive behavior or harm to consumers, they may investigate and block the transaction. The timeline and success of the merger, and thus arbitrage opportunities, might be impacted by delays or rejections by regulatory agencies.

Market risk: For me, this seems the greatest risk, because it is unquantifiable. Risk arbitrage (or "risk-arb") might be effective depending on prevailing market conditions. Changes in the target company's stock price due to unexpected market volatility or large market falls might have an impact on arbitrage positions. I've seen whole books of risk-arb positions collapse when a market becomes shaky and there is not much you can do about it either.

There are three ways you can be involved in risk-arb:

- Investing in the equities of the companies engaged in the M&A deal is a common strategy with professionals, and investment firms are built on it. Both the acquiring company and the acquired company can be involved here. Before a purchase is made, you can potentially make money by purchasing shares of the target firm as their price increases to the acquisition price or higher.
- Investors can practice merger arbitrage by purchasing shares of the acquired firm and short selling shares of the target company at the same time. The hope is to make a profit from the difference between the stock price of the target company and the acquisition price.
- Lastly, options. Investors can profit from M&A agreements by employing options tactics, such as purchasing call options on the target firm, or by putting options on the acquiring company. Investors can choose options that profit from either price hikes or price drops, depending on their outlook.

Recent successful M&A has included:

- **Aon and Willis Towers Watson:** Aon and Willis Towers Watson merged in March 2021 to create the world's largest professional services firm. The company provides a wide range of risk management, insurance brokerage and human capital solutions.
- **T-Mobile US and Sprint:** T-Mobile US and Sprint merged in April 2020 to create the third-largest wireless carrier in the United States. The merger has allowed the company to expand its network coverage and offer more competitive pricing.
- **Bristol-Myers Squibb and Celgene:** Bristol-Myers Squibb and Celgene merged in January 2020 to create one of the world's leading pharmaceutical companies. The merger has given the

company a broader pipeline of drugs and therapies, as well as a larger global footprint.

- **Dow Chemical and DuPont:** Dow Chemical and DuPont merged in August 2017 to create DowDuPont, a global leader in the materials science industry. The merger has allowed the company to combine its strengths and create new opportunities for growth.

Spin-offs

Spin-offs are my bread and butter. I've built a career on them. Full insight on spins is covered elsewhere in this book, but again ensure you quantify the risks first before investing. When a company decides to spin off a division or subsidiary as a separate publicly traded entity, it can create opportunities for investors. The rationale is that the spun-off company may be undervalued or overlooked by the market, leading to potential gains.

As well as market risk, which arguably is a risk in every investment, spin-off situation investments contain unique angles which, as an investor, you should take time to analyze. Remember, when you buy the parent company ahead of a spin-off, you will end up with two or more companies, and they may be of differing capital amounts, meaning you will have a weighting according to the spin-off ratio. This ratio will be found in the parent company's latest Form 10, which will give you various dates and timelines, including the ratio of the spin-off. Even if you have read up thoroughly on the filings and you are aware of what's coming and what you're getting, there are still a variety of risks that should be on your radar.

A lack of information: Assuming the parent company doing the spin is large enough, the spin-off company, which is usually (but not always) a lot smaller, will be in a different sector and, being a new company, will lack any sort of coverage. This is a two-edged sword. Spin-off companies may have limited historical financial data available to investors, making it challenging to assess their performance and potential, so getting your valuation ready can result in a great opportunity. Conversely, though, if most other investors have *not* done this, there can be wild early volatility. Remember, these are not IPOs. There is no set price to say what the spin-off should be listed at, and it continues essentially to be random.

Technical considerations: As mentioned, most spin-offs are smaller companies than the parent and usually the parent is a member of a particular index. When a spin-off occurs, the new entity might not immediately be included in the index. The index committee will decide based on the index's criteria, which might include market capitalization, liquidity and other factors. Calculating how much index selling or buying might occur can help you enormously with timing and, more importantly, avoiding short-term losses.

Examples of Spin-offs

There are usually 35–40 big spin-offs a year. Below are some of the more recent successful ones.

- General Electric Healthcare Technologies (GEHC) was spun off from General Electric (GE) in December 2021. GEHC is a leading provider of medical technology and digital health solutions. Stock price increase of GEHC since its spin-off: over 50%.
- Vertex Energy (VTNR) was spun off from Valero Energy (VLO) in November 2021. VTNR is a leading provider of renewable energy and refined products. Stock price increase of VTNR since its spin-off: over 30%.
- Confluent (CFLT) was spun off from Hortonworks (HDP) in June 2021. CFLT is a leading provider of cloud streaming data platforms. Stock price increase of CFLT since its spin-off: over 100%.
- Corteva (CTVA) was spun off from DowDuPont (DWDP) in June 2019. CTVA is a leading provider of agricultural chemicals and seeds. Stock price increase of CTVA since its spin-off: over 50%.
- Envista Holdings (NVST) was spun off from Danaher (DHR) in March 2019. NVST is a leading provider of dental and medical technology solutions. Stock price increase of NVST since its spin-off: over 100%.

Bankruptcies and Restructurings

Bankruptcy investing is not for the newbie. Before you embark down this route, you will need some financial savvy and some analytical number skills. Bankruptcy investing can be highly risky. Remember, a company filing for bankruptcy is an extremely sick company. A bankruptcy investment refers to the strategy of investing in the securities (stocks, bonds or other financial instruments) of a company that has declared bankruptcy or is undergoing bankruptcy proceedings. Investors make these bets because they expect the securities of troubled companies to trade at steep discounts to their true or future worth.

There are several convincing reasons why bankruptcy circumstances offer attractive investment opportunities. To begin, it is not uncommon for the securities of troubled corporations to trade at steep discounts, making assets available at prices below their true value. Overreactions in the market to bad news can cause prices to be off from their true worth, creating an opportunity for astute investors to profit.

The opportunity for reform and revival is an additional selling point. The value of a company's securities could increase significantly if it successfully reorganizes its debt and operations after filing for bankruptcy. The value of the company's tangible assets may provide investors with a way out, and a profit even if the business itself fails.

Moreover, for savvy investors, the uncertainty and nuance of bankruptcy cases might work to their favor. Expertise in the legal and financial systems is required, but those who have it can find untapped opportunities. Because of its unique characteristics, this market has less competition than others, which can improve your chances of making a profit. Bankruptcy investing is a technique best suited for people with extensive expertise and a high-risk tolerance due to its huge potential profits but also substantial risks.

Types of Bankruptcy Investments

Buying bonds or other debt securities from a bankrupt corporation at a deep discount is an example of distressed debt. Debt may be repaid at a better value than the acquisition price or converted to stock in the reformed company if the company is successful in its restructuring efforts.

Acquiring equity securities means investing in a bankrupt or failing company's stock. This is riskier, since equity shareholders are often the last to get any value in a bankruptcy action. However, if the company can emerge from bankruptcy and keep running, there is potential for significant gain.

A company's demise need not be immediate after filing for bankruptcy. There are numerous examples of organizations coming back from bankruptcy and becoming successful again. However, you should be aware of the dangers of filing for bankruptcy.

As a result of price increases and problems in their supply chain, global cosmetics giant Revlon filed for Chapter 11 bankruptcy in June 2022. After completing a successful reorganization, the company exited from bankruptcy in January 2023. Some of Revlon's less lucrative operations were shut down as part of the company's aim to reduce its debt by more than $3 billion. The business also received fresh funding from investors.

Other companies that have recently come out of bankruptcy:

- Hertz Global Holdings (2021)
- JCPenney (2020)
- Chesapeake Energy (2020)
- Neiman Marcus (2020)
- J. Crew (2020)

These companies have all faced significant challenges, but they have been able to restructure their businesses and emerge from bankruptcy stronger than before.

Rights Offerings

Rights offerings are interesting. By allowing existing shareholders to buy more shares at a discount, a publicly traded firm can generate more cash through a process known as a "rights offering". These can be looked at in a positive way, but generally the market may initially view them as negative.

- **Dilution**: A shareholder's ownership position in the company will be decreased if they do not participate in a rights offering. After the rights offering is finalized, their share of the company will be reduced.
- **A drop in worth**: If the stock price of the company drops following the rights offering, those who bought shares at the lower price may see a loss.
- **Participation cost:** The cost of taking part in a rights offering can be high. It's possible that shareholders will need to replenish their stockholdings by buying more shares.

These special situations are a little rarer, which is every reason to keep track of them. I like them because they are essentially forced sales, and any transaction that a company executes out of need instead of want should grab your attention. It does for me.

Examples of Rights Offerings

- The drugstore retailer Rite Aid (2017) used a rights offering to pay down some of its debt. Existing shareholders clearly have faith in the company, because the offering was oversubscribed.
- In order to help fund the purchase of Dollar Thrifty Automotive Group, Hertz Global Holdings (2013) held a rights offering. The offering was profitable and aided the firm's expansion plans.

- In 2010, Chesapeake Energy, a natural gas corporation, issued a rights offering to acquire funds and pay down debt. Investors welcomed the offering.
- To fortify its financial position during the economic downturn, General Electric (2008) resorted to a rights issue. This transaction was part of a larger capital-raising drive that also attracted participation from outside parties.
- In order to weather the storm of a tough retail climate, the department store chain Dillard's (2009) issued a rights offering. The money was used to improve the company's overall health and expand operations.
- In an effort to repay government bailout monies during the financial crisis, Citigroup (2009) conducted a rights offering. The bank was reorganizing its capital at the time of the offering.

The Proxy Contest

A proxy contest, also known as a "proxy battle" or "proxy fight", is a situation where a group of shareholders joins forces to gather enough shareholder proxies to win a corporate vote. This can be in opposition to the current management's intentions. These are a little more common in modern times, as they come from the rise of the activist investor. You might think that any big investor or group of investors that challenges the existing management are perceived as having a better vision. Not so fast. Many activist investors are just not that good. There are certain risks that come with a public fight, and these shouldn't be ignored if you are a shareholder.

- Neither the achievement nor the anticipated benefits of the activist's objective can be ensured.
- Proxy battles are inconvenient because they divert management's focus away from day-to-day operations.

- Both the company and the activist investors can incur significant costs during a proxy contest, and the shareholders may ultimately be responsible for covering those costs.
- Depending on the nature and visibility of the proxy battle, the market's perception of the company and the stock price could be negatively impacted.
- Shareholders can use proxy contests as a means of influencing the company's management and board and ensuring that their interests are being represented fairly. However, they can be acrimonious and cause the stock price of the company to fluctuate and be unpredictable throughout the time of the battle.
- In 2022, a hedge company called Elliott Management defeated the Chinese real estate giant Evergrande in a proxy struggle. With two seats on the board in their possession, Elliott Management pressured Evergrande to liquidate its assets and cut debt.
- A small activist hedge fund known as Engine No. 1 won three seats on ExxonMobil's board of directors in 2021. The triumph of Engine No. 1 was interpreted as evidence that shareholders are pressuring businesses to address climate change.
- The activist hedge fund Starboard Value prevailed in a 2019 proxy battle against Darden Restaurants, which owns chain restaurants like Olive Garden and LongHorn Steakhouse. Starboard Value was successful in replacing Darden Restaurants' entire board of directors, which led to the company selling assets and increasing profits.
- An activist investor named Nelson Peltz lost a proxy battle against Procter & Gamble in 2018. Nonetheless, Peltz's effort was effective in convincing Procter & Gamble to alter its business strategy, including the sale of assets and the enhancement of profitability.

CHAPTER 9

Less Obvious Special Situations You Should Look Out For

- → Navigating Economic Conditions
- → Reverse Morris Trusts
- → Initial Public Offerings
- → IPO Investment Checklist
- → Restructuring Strategies
- → Special Dividends
- → Share Buybacks
- → Tender Offers
- → Recapitalizations
- → Leveraged Buyouts

IN MY MANY discussions with fund managers over the years, I have often been told they "don't look at special situations," even when they look like a possible candidate. I've never really been able to pin down the exact reason. As an investor, you should be looking at every company you have and asking yourself, what is going to push price to value? Special situations are the perfect place to hunt for this. These situations can offer unique investment opportunities, but they can also be challenging to identify and capitalize on, for several reasons.

The financial, legal and operational details of special situations in the stock market are typically extensive. Investors need specific knowledge and ability to navigate these circumstances because of the complexities involved in understanding the intricacies and making predictions. The problem, though, is the dearth of relevant data. Many of these occurrences are not widely known, because they take place behind closed doors or because knowledge is only available to a small number of insiders. Furthermore, due to the fluid nature of these situations, they can undergo quick shifts. The projected trajectory can be altered by the appearance of new data or through unforeseen events, so investors must keep abreast of the latest developments and act fast.

Competition is fierce in the special situations market, with multiple institutional investors, hedge funds, and specialized investment firms all vying for the same openings. In situations like mergers and acquisitions, when the outcomes of regulatory assessments might be unpredictable, regulatory scrutiny further complicates an already difficult competitive landscape.

Another difficulty in today's information age is distinguishing between rumors and real, actionable intelligence. The short-lived nature of some of these possibilities also necessitates quick action from investors. Even though there is a greater potential for gain in exceptional circumstances, there is also a greater potential for loss. Investment losses are always a distinct risk if the actual results differ significantly from the predicted ones.

Navigating Economic Conditions

The perception that spin-offs or any other special situation continuously provide returns is a fallacy. Every situation carries risk and not least special situations. Sometimes, you can leverage these situations by looking at the wider picture.

Unpredictable cycles of prosperity and adversity are inherent to the business world, which is marked by economic shifts. Companies that excel in these circumstances can make rapid adjustments. Case studies provide valuable insights by highlighting businesses that adapted their strategies deftly in the face of economic volatility, whether through product diversification, market expansion, or cost-cutting measures.

Innovation and technology are crucial enablers of adaptability in this context, and keeping abreast of technological advancements is essential for competitiveness. Globalization amplifies the effects of economic shifts, necessitating increased adaptability from businesses with international operations. Significant roles in mitigating economic risks are played by effective risk management and the use of financial instruments. Government policies also influence economic shifts, requiring businesses that are subject to regulatory changes to remain vigilant.

Understanding and adapting to changing consumer behavior is another crucial aspect of successfully navigating economic shifts. This chapter segment equips readers with an understanding of the challenges and opportunities presented by economic fluctuations by emphasizing adaptability and providing real-world examples, and by highlighting adaptability's crucial role in thriving in the face of such uncertainty.

The main point is that, by taking in the wider landscape, special situations can be even more value creative. For example, I love spin-offs at the tops and the bottoms of markets because there is inherently something going on behind the scenes.

At tops of markets and full valuations of companies, the value of the spin-off could be much less than when the company spins off in distress. Each end of the spectrum can be an opportunity. I've said this time and time again, but work out the reason behind the situation. This is the key place to start. Value creation can come in many disguises and, while tax considerations are important in many equities' special situations, they are not the sole or primary factor driving these investment opportunities.

Reverse Morris Trusts

A Reverse Morris Trust (RMT) is a complex financial and tax strategy that businesses use when they want to sell a portion of their business or assets while paying as little tax as feasible. The primary objective of an RMT is to assist a company in disposing of obsolete assets while minimizing tax liability.

Imagine you have a collection of rare wines and wish to sell some bottles to a buddy, but you are eager to evade too high taxes. You start a new wine club and move the bottles there rather than marketing the wines straightforwardly. Then you give your friends shares in this new club in return for their unique wines. Your friend's wine club later on buys your club. Although this seems complicated, this strategy lets you sell your wines free from paying too much taxes.

This is done to ensure that companies can transfer portions of their business or assets without incurring significant tax losses. It's a clever way to keep more of their money when they make significant business adjustments.

The 2020 merger of Trane Technologies and Gardner Denver is a successful example of a recent RMT. Trane Technologies is a climate innovator that offers energy-efficient and environmentally responsible climate solutions for structures, homes and transportation. Gardner

Denver is a global champion in the provision of industrial technologies and solutions to a vast array of end markets.

Trane Technologies acquired Gardner Denver in a stock-for-stock transaction that was structured as a RMT. Gardner Denver shareholders received approximately 29% of the combined corporation, while Trane Technologies shareholders received approximately 71%.

The merger was beneficial for shareholders of both Trane Technologies and Gardner Denver. The shareholders of Trane Technologies benefited from the acquisition of a high-quality company with a strong history of expansion. Gardner Denver shareholders benefited from receiving stock in a larger, more diversified company with a solid financial standing.

Customers and workers also benefited from the merger. The merged company has a wider range of products and a larger global footprint, enabling it to better serve its consumers. Additionally, the merged company has a stronger financial position, allowing it to invest in new technologies and expansion initiatives.

In the Trane Technologies and Gardner Denver merger, the primary reason for the transaction was to create a more diversified and competitive company.

Initial Public Offerings

An initial public offering (IPO) is a big event for a company. It's when a company decides to sell its ownership to the public for the very first time. This means anyone, not just the company's founders or a few special investors, can buy a piece of the company by purchasing shares of its stock. They will go public for several reasons, the main one being to raise capital. For this reason, I tend not to like them.

Today, an IPO sadly has been reduced to a sale of a company at the highest possible price to raise the highest amount of money possible for the owner. Does that sound like a great investment to you? So, from that standpoint, they are manufactured investments, with all the current news flow priced in, that start with an uphill battle for the buyer to make a return.

- The marketing is geared to sell you the investment.
- Valuations are aimed towards the higher end.
- They only have one price to buy and no averaging, restricting value.
- Expiring lockout periods can cause the stock to fall.
- The investment is designed to benefit the seller.

Through the years, therefore, they have become less profitable, for a couple reasons. Firstly, the market achieves efficiency more quickly on a newly listed IPO than investors can. Secondly, the IPO's promoters tend to be more than liberal with the truth behind the offering in order to sell questionable valuations with slick marketing to an unsuspecting public.

It's time to move on from the IPO space if you are looking for newly listed growth companies without fluffy packaging. Spin-offs are the alternative and a better hunting ground for new companies, in my opinion.

I am a fan of the efficient-market hypothesis (EMH). The theory states that share prices reflect all information currently available. The EMH hypothesizes that stocks trade at their fair market value on exchanges, and all information available in the share price is factored in. It's not really a difficult theory to buy into, considering technology these days.

IPOs are designed to offer you an early entry into a new company (usually with huge supposed growth prospects). What started as a good idea has turned into a money-making machine not for the investor but for the founders and the investment banks that orchestrated the offering. A serious question you need to ask yourself before putting in your hard-earned cash: what is not priced in that the market doesn't know about?

An IPO Investment Checklist

If you are still thinking about investing, here is your checklist:

- **Hype and overvaluation:** IPOs, particularly those of well-known companies, can attract a lot of media attention and hype. This increased interest may cause the offered price to increase, which could result in overvaluation. Investors who invest early risk incurring a premium.
- **Lack of historical data:** Newly listed companies don't have a long history of financial disclosures to the public. It may be difficult to assess the company's performance and forecast its future course due to this lack of data.
- **First-day volatility:** Prices frequently see strong swings on the first trading day for stocks. For investors who desire consistency, such volatility can be unnerving.
- **Expiration of the lock-up period:** Following an IPO, early investors and insiders are frequently subject to a lock-up period during which they are normally unable to sell their shares. If many shares are sold in a short period of time after this, the stock price may decline.
- **Underperformance:** According to historical data, IPOs typically underperform the general market in the months and years after the offering. The chances of achieving significant long-term advantages can be skewed against, although there are undoubtedly exceptions.
- **Investment banks and insiders:** These parties may have interests that diverge from those of the typical investor. Investment banks underwrite IPOs. Rather than creating long-term value for new shareholders, their objective might be to secure a successful offering.
- **Pressure on management:** After a firm becomes public, the management team is under more pressure to reach quarterly targets. Sometimes, long-term growth efforts are hampered by this short-term focus.

- **Unproven management:** In some instances, the management group of a firm going public may not have prior experience managing a publicly traded company, which has its own unique set of difficulties and legal requirements.
- **Economic and market conditions:** A freshly public company's performance may be impacted by general economic issues and market conditions. The stock may decline if a firm goes public during a bull market, but the economy deteriorates soon after.
- **Diluted shares:** Shares may be diluted because of future equity funding rounds or the exercise of stock options, which will affect early investors.

Restructuring Strategies

Split-offs and carve-outs are two strategies companies use to restructure their business, each with its own distinct approach and implications for the company and its shareholders.

Split-Offs

A split-off is a corporate reorganization where a parent company allows shareholders to exchange their shares for those in a subsidiary, detaching the subsidiary from the parent firm. This diminishes the parent company's outstanding shares since shareholders must give up their parent shares to get subsidiary shares. Split-offs optimize operations, focus on key business areas, or uncover subsidiary value. Shareholders and companies frequently benefit from tax-free transactions.

Split-offs have pros and cons for investors. They give the possibility to invest in a more focused company, which may unleash hidden wealth as the market revalues the split entities based on their merits, increasing shareholder value. This realignment lets investors spend money strategically based on each entity's prospects. Split-offs are usually tax-efficient, preserving shareholder value.

The downsides include limited liquidity as stockholders may hold shares in a smaller, less traded corporation. To appropriately appraise the new business without a past independent financial track record could lead to volatility or underperformance if the market's expectations are not realized. Thus, split-offs can be rewarding, but investors must assess the dangers.

Exchange offers and split-offs are separate but complementary ideas. An exchange offer is a method by which one firm can acquire some of the shares of another company that has been formed through a split-off. In doing so, the acquiring firm may be able to increase its influence over the newly formed entity. A lot of situations, including mergers and acquisitions, can involve exchange offers, so it's vital to keep that in mind.

Carve-Outs

A carve-out occurs when a parent company sells part of a subsidiary or division's shares to the public via an IPO or a private investor. Carve-outs, unlike split-offs, leave the parent business with controlling ownership in the subsidiary, which becomes a legal entity with publicly traded stock.

Carve-outs can increase value realization when the market evaluates the spun-off organization, typically revealing undervalued business elements. They offer fresh investment options, especially IPOs, allowing investors to diversify and support industry leaders. Parent companies can raise capital through carve-outs to pay down debt, reinvest in core activities, or restore value to shareholders.

Carve-outs can be risky, especially if the new business struggles to establish its independence or operate without the parent corporation. The parent firm and newly independent entity's stock values may fluctuate throughout the separation. If the newly created firm lacks scale, market presence, or financial stability, investors may be less interested. Thus, while carve-outs might provide high-reward opportunities, investors must handle volatility and the hurdles of assessing the new entity's standalone chances.

VMware, a global leader in cloud infrastructure and digital workspace technology, was carved out by Dell Technologies in 2021. Dell paid off a large chunk of its debt and VMware was allowed to explore strategic relationships and development prospects independently. The market initially welcomed this carve-out since it unlocked shareholder value for Dell and gave VMware more cloud computing agility.

Special Dividends

A firm may give a special dividend to its shareholders, which is separate from its usual payouts. In order to repay extra capital to shareholders, companies often offer special dividends. This can happen following a business unit sale, a lucrative period or a major capital structure change.

They give you instant income and maybe even tax breaks, but they may also mean that there aren't any chances to reinvest, which could mean that the business is mature or growing slowly. When a special dividend is announced, it can be good for the stock price. However, buyers should be aware of how the share price will change after the dividend and how the tax consequences may be different from capital gains taxation.

Before deciding, you should carefully think about why a business is giving a special dividend and what that means for the company's future. You should also make sure that the special dividend fits with your investment strategy.

Share Buybacks

Buybacks are very important for you as an investor. The announcement and execution of a buyback offers multiple financial and psychological benefits. Companies and investors alike can reap many rewards from these events. They boost earnings per share by lowering the number of outstanding shares, which shows that management is confident in the stock's worth and could cause its price to rise.

Companies can take advantage of favorable market conditions without committing to regular payouts like dividends through buybacks, giving shareholders more flexibility in returning value. Because capital gains are often subject to a lower tax rate than dividend income, they also provide investors with tax efficiency.

In addition to enhancing financial ratios and reducing the dilution effect from issuing new shares, buybacks can eliminate excess cash that is not necessary for immediate operations. Active buybacks by corporations can help investors optimize their portfolios, meaning they can increase the value of their assets without having to make any changes to their portfolio.

Tender Offers

Tender offers provide investors the chance to buy shares directly at a price above the market rate. This permits investors to sell their shares at a premium and signals to the market that the acquirer believes the firm is undervalued, which may induce a re-evaluation. Furthermore, tender offers give stockholders a liquidity event and an appealing exit route. Investors like such offerings because they can provide rapid profit and a strategic exit.

Recapitalizations

A recapitalization is a business move that changes the balances of a company's debt and stock to stabilize or improve its capital structure. This technique is important to investors for various reasons. For starters, it can improve the company's financial health, by either reducing overall debt or refining the debt-to-equity ratio, perhaps improving the company's credit status.

Furthermore, recapitalization frequently seeks to release cash that can be given as dividends to shareholders, so directly benefiting them financially. Furthermore, it can cause a transfer in control or ownership, potentially revealing hidden value within the organization. These strategic financial adjustments are critical, providing avenues for higher firm valuations and shareholder returns.

Leveraged Buyouts

In a leveraged buyout (LBO), the buyer mostly uses borrowed money to pay for a deal, putting up the assets of both the target and buying company as security for the loans. There are several reasons why buyers are interested in LBOs. To begin with, they usually involve many changes to how the company is run and how much money it makes. The organization hopes that these alterations will increase productivity and revenue.

It's riskier to use this way because you must take on more debt, but it might pay off big in the end. When the acquired company's debt is gradually paid off, investors may get a lot of money back if an LBO is good. Also, if the market thinks the LBO is a smart move to make things run more smoothly or if they think the price paid is fair, they may react positively. This can increase investor interest and possibly increase shareholder value.

Summary of Why These Situations Are Important

Tender offers, recapitalizations and LBOs are examples of exceptional situations that investors should keep an eye on since they might provide unique value possibilities that aren't always easy to find in the regular market. Dealing with unique circumstances requires a deep comprehension of the intricacies of finance, law and operations.

These conditions also present opportunities for great return, with increased risk and competition. The economy and how well a company can respond to changing market conditions are also very important. You can find great opportunities in companies that can quickly shift their strategies in response to these changes. There are a lot of things to think about and choices to make when it comes to your holdings or potential holdings.

For instance, RMTs provide tax-efficient disposals, while IPOs offer growth opportunities but also risks, such as overvaluation and a lack of historical data. Furthermore, astute investors can take advantage of opportunities presented by corporate change activities such as split-offs and carve-outs, which can drastically change a company's structure and market value. Investors who want to take advantage of unique opportunities to make money must have a firm grasp of these dynamics.

PART THREE

WIDER THOUGHTS ABOUT INVESTING

CHAPTER 10

Finding an Edge in Your Investing

- → Finding an Edge in Your Investment
- → Why Owning Spin-offs Are a Great Reward Vs Risk

LEGENDARY MILITARY TACTICIAN Sun Tzu changed the way that war and warfare are conducted today. Not much is known about him with certainty, but he is best known for *The Art of War*, a work that serves as a manual for winning wars and conflicts.

"Therefore, those who win every battle are not really skilled – those who render others' armies useless without fighting are the best of all," Sun Tzu wrote. This "fighting without fighting" is much more of a mental contest than an actual physical fight.

The same holds true in investing.

The stock market is always difficult. First understanding it and then thinking of a smarter way to beat it can not only provide returns but also help you sleep at night. Never underestimate a good night's sleep!

When I started our research firm in 2007, we simply analyzed spin-offs. We took a generic name for the firm, but as we grew, we morphed into a company that analyzed many different areas of public investments and found ourselves being very opportunistic in our thinking.

We needed a new name and brand and employed a PR firm to help us figure it out.

I remember sitting down in the UK with Berkeley Communications and their CEO Chris Hewitt. After an extensive exercise and brainstorming session, and with the many questions he threw at me, I kept repeating the fact that the gold dust in any investment was to have a unique angle and to ensure that this was paramount to successful returns.

Finally, our new firm, The Edge, was born.

It's more than just a name. It is my core belief, and it expresses my purpose. It was what was inside me that I felt passionate about, and Chris was smart enough to spot that. I wanted to help investors make a return by helping them think about potential investments differently. To this day, I maintain my passionate belief that investors need an edge.

It may seem that you have a mountain to climb here. How are you going to come up with an edge, and where do you start?!

Finding an Edge in Your Investment

Sometimes it's more than just picking a good stock – you'd be surprised, most can. Instead, I will give you some insights gained from my many years that can add a safety net to your process, which is essential if you are going to gain an edge. Never forget, this is an odds game. You will be rewarded not only by placing your bets with the signposts pointing in the correct direction, but by managing the losses when things don't go as planned.

Expect to have periods where you will lose. The latter is more important than the former, because most people find it hard to accept that they were wrong. This leads to losses outstripping profits. Therefore, most do not stand the test of time.

Markets Price in Everything

Markets are broadly efficient. The Efficient Market Hypothesis (EMH) states that share prices reflect all information and consistent alpha generation is impossible.

For this reason, it should be impossible to outperform the overall market through expert stock selection or market timing. The only way an investor can obtain higher returns is by purchasing riskier investments. Well, after all this time in the market, I can tell you there are ways of beating it.

- Proponents of EMH posit investors benefit from investing in a passive portfolio.

- Opponents of EMH believe it is possible to beat the market and stocks can deviate from their fair market prices.

What Drives Markets Short Term?

In 2020, nearly 24 million new investors came to the market, fueled by government stimulus and nowhere else to put their money (because of the pandemic). These new investors inflated the stock market. When it comes to stocks, human instinct is to buy, which added up to a huge rally of stocks that these newbies just "liked".

The meme generation was born. It was, in other words, a bubble, but as with any bubble it's instructive to think about what went wrong and what to do afterwards. In 2002, the S&P took 12 years to gain similar levels. Roughly 90% of internet stocks went to zero. In 2008, it took four years. There is good reason to believe that this market will not recover for a while, but let's look at the driving forces.

Emotions:

- As humans, we are driven by emotion, genetics, stress and diet
- Mr Market has a way of moving things around
- There are heightened expectations of supply, demand and expected company performance

Crowd behavior:

- Fear of missing out (FOMO): that anxious feeling you get when you think other people might be making money when you're not
- Asset bubbles, meme stocks, r/WallStreetBets, and other subreddits
- Herd behavior: groups rush in

Fear and greed:

- "Be fearful when others are greedy, and greedy when others are fearful." – Warren Buffett

- Common intuition states that, in a fearful market people are looking to irrationally sell stock, and in a greedy market people are looking to buy
- Fear and greed have their place in financial bubbles.

Long term, if you have carried out your thesis correctly, your plan works. You must manage the short-term drivers in between.

The Psychology of Movement in Markets

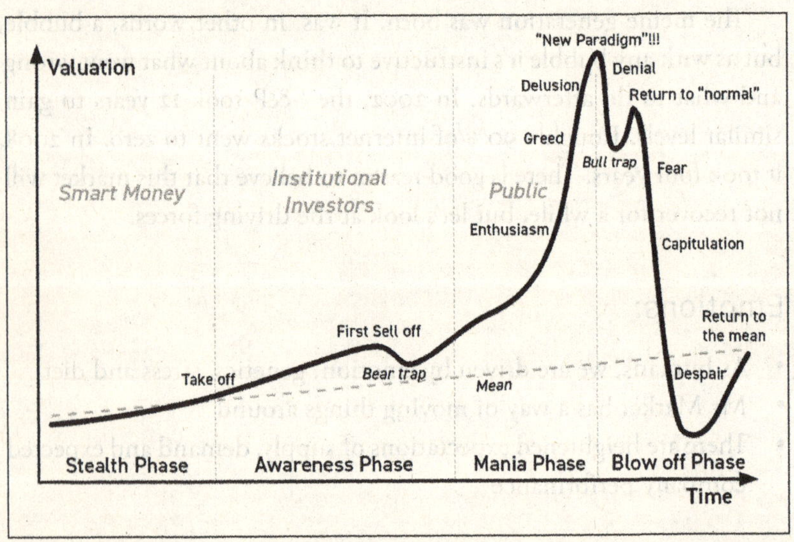

The key to long-term success is defining your edge in the market. Most investors think they know how to beat the market. They analyze macro implications, look at money flows, options flows, the VIX, follow social media, read blogs, etc., but you need to work out how you out-think the market.

Your behavior is probably the most overlooked determinant to achieving better results than anyone else. The disciplined investor with a process, risk management, and definable edge will outperform the majority over the long term every day of the week. The irrational one wins sometimes, but this just boils down to luck. Sorry to break that to some of you.

The good news is that there are only three types of edge to choose from.

Let's look at these now.

The Three Ways to Make Money (or The Three Types of Edge)

When it comes down to it, there really are only three ways of making money as an investor and thus three types of edge:

1. Insider Information

Knowing something about a future event in a company that no one else does, you choose to invest ahead of it. In 2004, Martha Stewart sold 4000 shares of ImClone (a biotech firm). Two days later, the stock fell 16% after it was publicly announced that the FDA had not approved its primary pharmaceutical product, Erbitux. She served five months in prison, plus five months of home confinement. Clearly, this is not a viable edge.

2. Faster Dissemination of Information

Execute on information faster than anyone else. Sadly, the internet and technology will always get there faster than you, meaning you have lost before you started. Most people don't have an informational edge. You can have better information than everyone else, but it usually disappears quickly because it tends to be extremely short-term in nature. High-speed trading algorithms will beat you every time. So this is not viable either.

3. Smarter Analysis

Be smarter and look where few other people are looking. Undercovered corporate events that are announced but haven't happened yet are a true and tested source of returns. This is my edge.

The Analytical Edge

Essentially, to be successful, you only have one way to make money and that's smarter analysis. I like to divide this into two complementary parts: outthinking the market (*analytical edge*) and controlling your emotions (*behavioral edge*).

An analytical edge allows you to see the same information everyone else sees, but you see it in a different light. After 25 years of looking at spin-offs and other special situations, managing money and producing research has enabled me to see things through a quality–value filter.

The information I use is public – available to anyone. I just have the experience of looking at it in a certain way.

Maybe you have more experience with a certain company or a certain type of business. Maybe you see risk differently.

Your edge allows you to weigh the information more effectively and get to a point where you think there could be a potential move away from price to value, which leads you to a different probability of the investment's outcome.

Use as many tools as you can to do this – but make sure they contribute to your edge.

Behavioral Edge

The behavioral edge has two parts. The first is knowing that behavioral biases exist and can be exploited in markets. You need to know how different biases affect asset prices, where they can be found and when they can be exploited. Hence the popular phrase "buy when others are selling".

The second part is knowing that you are just as susceptible to these biases as everyone else. That includes overconfidence. Humans tend to overestimate their abilities on the upside and be overly pessimistic on the downside. Rarely do things play out as badly as people's pessimism leads them to think. Thus the phrase "This will end in disaster", when it rarely ever does.

This kind of thinking can lead to a depressive outlook on the world. The tendency to overemphasize the negative can have an impact on the choices we make and the risks we are willing to take. This is the principle behind why "bad news sells". A truism is that surrounding yourself with doomsayers can make you despondent about the future.

Knowing how you react to asset price changes and extreme market swings is more important than chasing a holy grail strategy that doesn't exist. Smart investing is about looking in the right places and behaving better than everyone else.

CHAPTER 11

Short Selling

- → Warning: Shorts Can Kill You
- → Enter The Greater Fool Theory
- → A Short Guide to Buying Stocks
- → The Time Problem
- → Math
- → Unexpected News
- → Earnings
- → A Case Study

Warning: Shorts Can Kill

"SHORT SELLING" AND the concept of selling something you don't own is very complicated and may blow your mind. Of all strategies, "going short" on a stock is one of the riskiest actions you can take. It should be approached with great caution, for newbies and professionals alike. If executed correctly, it can be a significant part of your special situation armory, but it should be used very carefully and sparingly.

Going short can potentially make you a lot of money. The short sale is the expectation of a reduction in the price of an asset in the belief that you will be able to buy it back cheaper later. Remember, if most investors hold stocks, betting on an alternative direction, and indeed an unexpected outcome, can be highly rewarded by the market.

Selling something you don't own is not new; many people have done it and got it right, but, importantly, many have got it wrong too.

The most famous and successful currency short in history immortalized Hungarian-American billionaire George Soros. His strategy of short selling the British pound (GBP) was a master stroke. The UK government was caught in a battle with the European Union over currency, and "Black Wednesday" on 16 September 1992 forced the UK government to pull out of the European Exchange Rate Mechanism (ERM).

Ultimately, the pound fell sharply, and Soros pocketed $1 billion, instantly making him an enemy of the British state and garnering him the moniker "The Man Who Broke the Bank of England".

Enter the Greater Fool Theory

The concept of selling assets that are not their true worth is especially prevalent right now. Take digital asset Bitcoin, which has given investors a white-knuckle ride. It has seen unprecedented volatility, rocketing up and down for years.

In March 2010, it was worth $0.003; just seven years later, on 17 December 2017, its value was $19,783.06, while on its 10th anniversary on 31 October 2018, its price was $6,300 and in December 2019 was $7,294.

But crucially, it has no material value. There is fundamentally no reason for it being at any price, but it is. There is a camp that says, "I will never invest" and believe it should be worth zero, and others who will support it at any price it dictates – the higher the better. We will go into more detail about cryptocurrencies later in the book.

With stocks, you can add up numbers and metrics and finally get to a value. That value is its fair price. When stocks deviate from that price, investors buy if it's cheap or sell if it's expensive. With Bitcoin, there is no way of knowing what that fair value is. It's trading at what investors believe it's worth.

Taken at face value, you could say the same about stocks. They trade at what investors believe they are worth. Just because they are trading above or below their fair price doesn't necessarily mean the stock will rise or fall on that basis.

There are many cases of stocks remaining cheap forever and expensive stocks staying that way too. It's the perception of what an asset is worth that gives rise to a concept that Berkshire Hathaway CEO Warren Buffett often cites. His claim that Mr Market determines the price is spot on – they don't call him the Oracle of Omaha for nothing!

The perception of an asset's worth reminds me of a story from the 17th century, which still resonates to this day. Tulip mania, which swept Holland from 1634 to 1637, is widely believed to be the world's first speculative bubble.

The hysteria of tulip bulb buying took the country by storm, sparking interest from rich and poor alike. At one point, the price of a bulb reached 7000 guilders, more than ten times the average worker's salary and more expensive than an opulent canal-side home in Amsterdam.

The phenomenon developed further when traders began buying and selling contracts for the next season's bulbs without ever seeing them. They entered futures contracts, with the physical bulbs not changing hands.

In November 1636, the craze began to reach its peak until finally, in February 1637, after prices spiked by 1100%, the market collapsed suddenly at a bulb auction in Haarlem, when buyers refused to pay the inflated prices.

Over a period of one week, it is said bulbs lost 90% of their value, leading to widespread panic and causing massive losses to those left holding the contracts. It led to a loss of trust in the commodities market for many years.

A Short Guide to Buying Stocks

Now let's turn our attention to buying stocks. "Going long" is what you do when you have faith that the company and management will deliver its promises and ultimately provide a return for shareholders that will materialize in a rise in the share price – hopefully, a lot higher than what was paid.

"Going short" is the exact opposite. You favor a fall in the share price, perhaps because you see a decline in the business, and you essentially sell shares you do not own. You profit when you buy the shares back cheaper than when you sold them.

When approaching any sort of investment, my mindset is: how much can I lose versus what am I realistically expected to gain. That should be yours too – in other words, risk versus reward. Investors sometimes get carried away by fantastic money-making stories, but it's here that you should keep your head.

When you buy a stock long, your downside is limited, because it can only ever go to zero. The problem with the short-selling strategy is: if you sell the shares short and the shares go up, you must return them to the lender, buying them back at a higher price, which will result in a loss. So the downside is unlimited, which is why this could be a very risky strategy. Your risk versus reward is 100% gain versus unlimited loss.

There are three things to remember when shorting stocks:

1. Assets can take a long time to come down.
2. The math of short selling isn't in your favor.
3. Unexpected positive news will hurt you.

The Time Problem

Let's deal with timing. I often say around the office, and in general, that everyone is right; it's just a matter of timing. This is very true in the stock market, because it's so driven by emotion.

Even big guys, like Bill Ackman of Pershing Square, are driven by emotion. Ackman's condemnation of Herbalife (HLF), the nutrition company he declared as a pyramid scheme in December 2012, was motivated by passion.

His presentation at the Sohn Conference in New York was legendary. He opened with a 342-slide presentation and argued the case for zero. A slide read: "Participants in the Herbalife scheme, the distributors, obtain their monetary benefits primarily from recruitment rather than the sale of goods and services to the consumer."

But the price continued to rise, and Ackman spent the following five years engaged in a ferocious war of words, not only with Herbalife but with his peers, including the icon Carl Icahn, who opened an opposing short, just to spite him.

In July 2016, the Federal Trade Commission fined Herbalife $200 million after an investigation but stopped short of calling it a pyramid scheme. It ordered the firm to restructure, and in January

2017, announced that the 350,000 victims of Herbalife's multi-level marketing scheme would be refunded.

In February 2018, Ackman revealed he'd closed his position and his public appearances diminished. The loss of an estimated $1 billion sent investors rushing for the exit, and his ego took a bashing.

At the time of writing, Herbalife's share price has fallen to the price Ackman shorted it at.

In my experience, the problem with shorts is they don't normally happen in the time frame you want them to. For whatever reason, emotion plays a bigger part when people discuss shorts. Those who are shorting want you to know that they know something you don't, and what's more, their esoteric knowledge is far superior.

But keep in mind, the thought of losing an infinite amount can play havoc with your mental health. Just be extremely careful on shorts. Having no boundary (as when you are long) is a tricky one for the brain. We are emotional creatures, after all.

Math

When you short a stock, it must come from somewhere, and they are essentially "borrowed" from a broker. The end owner is usually a pension fund, a mutual fund, or another investor. If you have a short position, you will most certainly be paying borrowing costs to the lender.

Something to be aware of if you have a book of shorts is: the harder to borrow, the higher the cost. Financing costs will eat into any possible profit. Secondly, the short sales' total profit is bounded by zero, by which I mean it's the most you'll ever make. That's quite a tall order, as something significant will have to happen in order to make the stock go to zero. This is usually fraud, but in today's world, I find it's quite difficult for a company to cook the books for any length of time (though this is not to say that it isn't possible, because it is). On the downside, your losses are unlimited, and you could pay anything to close out your short.

Unexpected News

Unexpected news is the greatest unknown risk you will have to your short. When I managed money, it kept me awake at night. Every night, in fact. I'd check the news flow on my shorts twice as often as my longs.

Strong, positive news on a short could wipe out your quarter or even your year. Positive news could come on several fronts, but I'll point you in the direction of a few things you should be aware of before you short that stock.

Remember, if you are shorting a stock because it's weak, there could be companies circling and looking to take advantage of this weakness. You will need to evaluate and analyze your takeover risk with any name you short.

Investors are smarter than ever before, and a good company going through a bad patch (which it potentially can come out of) isn't a great short candidate.

The company could even realize this themselves and announce a tie-up or merger, sending the stock soaring. Some of these investors could be activist investors, and I know that at The Edge we look for companies that are being managed badly and in a state of weakness.

In today's stock markets, the major stockholders come in the form of passive investors. There is an exchange-traded fund (ETF) for everything and every index. If the market goes up, the ETF (and consequently your stock) will go up. A bull market with the algorithmic traders could force you out of that position. Let's face it, history shows that stock markets generally appreciate, although this is a bit of a generalization.

Earnings

Stocks don't usually move on earnings. They move on expectation. I often read headlines that say "good earnings" or "strong sales". We live in a relative world, and stocks will move according to what is expected.

Never forget this. Notice the language, and remember, you should look at what is expected and what has happened. That will determine any move in the stock price.

Also, companies that are in distress may announce restructuring, change of management, or even a break-up. Perceptions of a problem being solved can provide an uplift to the stock, which in turn will hurt your short. Complete structural changes may turn it around entirely.

Watch for changes in fundamentals on your short positions. Our natural "buying" brain likes to own things; this could be anything from stocks to cars to houses. We are not natural sellers or, moreover, short sellers of anything.

Deterioration in or bad news about a company usually causes a stock to move violently on the downside, which results in fear and more selling as the longs try to liquidate. The potential payoff can be hugely attractive, not to mention lucrative, on the basis that you are in the minority.

Lately, investors have made a high profile of short selling. These include Bill Ackman of Pershing Square, Jim Chanos of Kynikos Associates, and David Einhorn of Greenlight Capital.

Case Study: Varex Imaging Corporation

In July 2019, interesting data was released on the Varex Imaging Corporation (VREX), which got me thinking. The Utah-based firm is a leading independent supplier of medical X-ray tubes and image processing solutions. From medical imaging to cargo screening and border security, their components are used by global X-ray imaging system manufacturers. So, we started digging, firstly on the fundamentals.

Kevin Yankton, VREX's Chief Accounting Officer (CAO), sold shares twice (accounting for 100% of his holdings) on the open market during the month of July 2019. Yankton sold 1149 shares (at $31) on 15 July 2019 (totaling $35,619), and later sold 268 shares (at $30.56) on 5 July 2019 (totaling $8,190).

These stake sales were performed under Rule 10b5-1, which designates a planned sale, and Yankton initiated these sales on 5 June 2019. Nothing too suspicious about that, you may say!

Well, it initially concerned me on two fronts. Firstly, Yankton was the money man. If anyone knew how the company was doing, it was him. Secondly, selling everything he owned while sitting on the board was worrying. We kept digging.

It wasn't a particularly unique business off the bat. I like businesses that have an edge and some sort of barrier to their entry. VREX sold its products to a limited number of original equipment manufacturers, many of which are also its competitors with in-house X-ray component manufacturing operations.

VREX's top five customers (by revenue) collectively contributed 37% in FY18, with VREX's top ten customers accounting for 49% of revenue in the same period. Additionally, VREX's largest customer, Canon Medical Systems Corp (a subsidiary of Canon, Inc., 7751 JP), solely added 18% to revenues in FY18.

Therefore, we believed the loss of one or more of VREX's top customers would have a material and adverse effect on its profitability. This was the first risk. Secondly, this was an industry characterized by rapidly evolving technology, intense competition, and frequent pricing pressure.

Lastly, and more recently, the US was going through a trade war with China. VREX derived 10% of its revenues from China, with the intent to increase China-based revenue due to the government's expansion plans.

However, over the last several years, the US had implemented new tariffs on steel, aluminum and many other goods, most relevantly key raw materials that VREX imported from China. This had been a significant factor impacting its gross margins, which had been reduced from roughly 40% in FY16 to around 33% in FY18.

The US–China trade implications potentially had more damaging effects on the company. While planned sales of companies are usually set up to avoid accusations of insider trading by selling a predetermined number of shares at a predetermined time, what made this unusual was (i) the complete removal of shares, (ii) being performed by an officer versus a director, (iii) he previously sold at a higher level ($37) and (iv) the timing ahead of earnings on 6 August 2019.

Previously, Yankton sold 862 shares (at $37) on 14 May 2018 (totaling $31,894) under the same Rule 10b5-1, which he initiated on the same day, only 11 days after VREX's Q2 2018 earnings. Following the Q3 2018 earnings report on 2 August 2018, shares dropped 26% on the day.

VREX, Russell 2000, July 2018 to July 2019

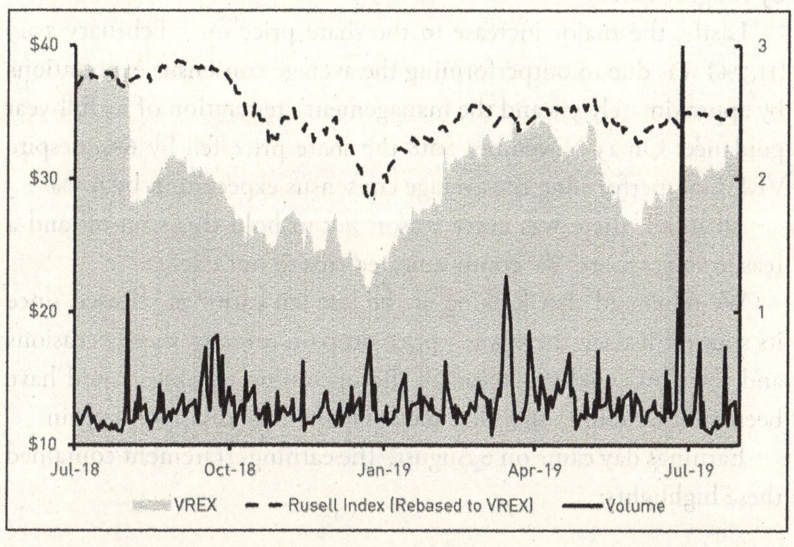

So, on the face of it, the fundamentals weren't good. There was also the risk that they might get worse. VREX has a net leverage ratio of 2.9x FY18, which is higher than its peers' average leverage ratio of 1.9x. Furthermore, VREX has a lower adjusted EBITDA margin of around 14% in FY18 compared to its average peers' margin of 20%.

Then we looked a little deeper. VREX announced ten quarterly earnings following its spin-off separation from Varian Medical

Systems, Inc. (VAR). We examined the market reactions after each of these earnings and noted the price drops outweighed the rallies, with earnings resulting in seven declines compared to only three increases.

Notably, the major declines appeared on 2 August 2018 and 1 February 2018, with drops of 26.3% and 20.3%, respectively. In terms of positive movement, VREX saw the sharpest increase to its share price on 5 February 2019, surging 11.7%.

The primary reason for the decline on 2 August 2018 (26.3%) was the cut in revenue guidance to 8% to 10% from the earlier projection of 13% to 14%. The rationale behind the decline on 1 February 2018 (20.3%) was VREX falling short of expected mean consensus revenue by roughly 10%.

Lastly, the major increase to the share price on 5 February 2019 (11.7%) was due to outperforming the average consensus expectations by approximately 5% and the management's reiteration of its full-year guidance. On 13 November 2018 the share price fell by 6%, despite VREX outperforming the average consensus expectation by 6.3%.

All in all, there was every reason *not* to hold this spin-off and a reason to go short. We communicated this to our clients.

We reiterated that looking at the last ten earnings released since its spin-off listing, there was a price drop on seven of those occasions, and the CAO's selling ahead of the upcoming earnings could have been another telling sign that the company may disappoint again.

Earnings day came on 6 August. The earnings statement contained these highlights:

- Revenues increased 3% to $197 million
- Gross margin was 31% | Adjusted gross margin was 34%
- Operating earnings margin was 2% | Adjusted operating earnings margin was 9%
- Net earnings were $(0.04) per diluted share | Adjusted net earnings were $0.24 per diluted share.

"Our business had solid gains in revenues in the third quarter, and operating earnings comparable to the prior year quarter. Quarterly revenues were up 3% led by record-level global CT tube sales and double-digit sales growth in products for the oncology and mammography imaging markets. The Direct Conversion acquisition we completed early in the third quarter contributed approximately $2 million of revenues, as expected, and integration activities are well underway. Offsetting these revenue gains were significantly lower sales of radiographic detectors," said Sunny Sanyal, Chief Executive Officer of Varex.

VREX, S&P 500, rebased to VREX, July 2018 to July 2019

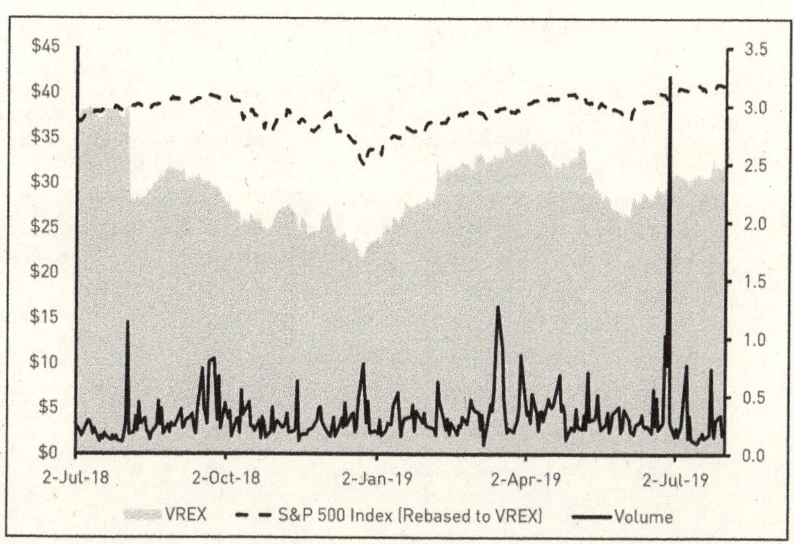

In the third quarter, Varex recorded $7 million restructuring and impairment charges in connection with the recently announced plans to close its Santa Clara facility. These charges, as well as higher tax expense, contributed to a net loss for the quarter.

Reads well, doesn't it? The stock fell 20%; they missed estimates on adjusted net income and adjusted earnings per share.

Whether you are shorting stock or just selling your holding, it's essential to have constant screening on your stocks and new ideas. It's also a good lesson into why you should *always* investigate the fundamentals of your holdings to identify red flags, before you commit.

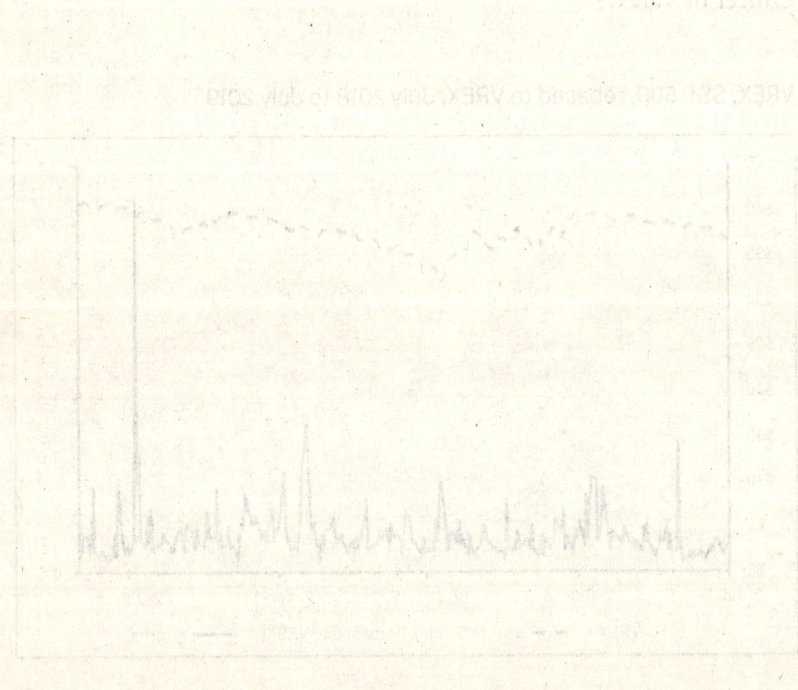

CHAPTER 12

Mastering Market Volatility

- 10 Tactical Portfolio Protection Strategies
- Diversification
- Keeping High Quality Investments
- Inflation-Resistant Investments
- Regular Rebalancing
- Assess Your Portfolio's Risk Tolerance
- Staying Informed
- Fixed Income Allocation
- Hedging with Options
- Stress Testing
- Long-term Perspective

THE VIX, OR VOLATILITY INDEX, quantifies investor uncertainty about the direction of the S&P 500 in the next 30 days. It is also known as the "fear index", since it rises when investors are apprehensive about the market. A low VIX score suggests that investors do not anticipate significant volatility, whereas a high VIX reading implies that they do. A VIX rating of ten or less is considered low, while one of 20 or more is considered high.

For retail investors tracking market emotion, the VIX can be a useful tool. If the VIX rises, it may imply that investors are growing increasingly anxious and that the market is becoming more volatile. At the time of writing, the VIX had been declining in recent weeks. As of 12 August 2023, the VIX was trading at 15.96, which was down from a high of 21.77 in July 2023.

There are several good reasons why the VIX went down. First, the stock market has been quiet over the past few weeks. The S&P has been trading in a narrow band, and there have been no big drops. Because of this, some buyers are less afraid of the market. But are we all getting a little too comfortable? Stubborn inflation, the possibility of a recession, rising interest rates and geopolitical tensions are all reasons you should think about protecting your portfolio after a good run this year.

When a market or stock rallies and you are sitting on a profit, the tendency is to look to sell. The fear of losing gains is one of the most powerful emotions that can drive the liquidation of positions. When the value of an investment has increased, investors may be concerned that the profits will be lost if they do not lock them in. Fear of losing what they've earned can lead to rash sales.

Protecting Your Portfolio

So, let's assume (and this is a big assumption) that you have narrowed down and gained control over your emotional biases. How, in practical terms, can you protect your portfolio?

The stock market's prices naturally fluctuate due to a variety of reasons, such as economic indicators and market mood. Stock price changes that are sudden and severe, or even the expectation of the same, can cause us to be concerned, and this increases volatility.

There are so many things to worry about in today's world. What are the main issues, and how do you separate that from what is happening rather than what may or may not happen? Incidentally, according to research, many of the disasters that investors are concerned about are statistically unlikely to occur. The frequency of recurrence of certain unfavorable events is often less than people's sense of how frequently they occur.

I tend to deal with problems as they occur rather than worrying about what may or may not happen. I believe this makes me a better investor.

The stock market never ceases to amaze me with the fact that it continues to fool investors and, really, that is down to swaying your emotions. Some investors are more emotional than others, and this will cause them to make decisions they wouldn't normally make, that will cause them to lose money. Gaining control of your emotions starts with an evaluation of the facts. It's too easy to just say, "Get control." Most investors, and even I, as a seasoned one, will find it difficult sometimes.

If you are worried today about the possible effects of a meltdown in the stock market, as it seems many are, make a list of what you are worried about and see what practical things you can do to negate that worry, other than selling everything. Remember, your mind will try to rule you, and your biases may influence your decisions. Stick to the facts.

Not being in the market is never an option for me. Fine tuning the portfolio is a long-term compounder. Remember all that hard work you've put in to take a position? There is nothing worse than seeing the market force you out because you sold on emotion only to discover the stock flies thereafter.

Yes, we've all been there. Maintain a long-term investment perspective and avoid making rash judgments based on short-term market swings. Markets tend to rebound over time, even after bouts of turbulence. When all hell is breaking loose, think forward a bit longer than a day or a week.

Ten Tips to Negate Risks

The following are ten ways in which you can negate risks in your portfolio and lean on the facts rather than the emotional brain. The strategies come with a caveat. Regularly assessing your portfolio's risk tolerance and making changes based on your financial goals and changing market conditions is an ongoing and periodic exercise.

A portfolio tailored to your risk tolerance might help you stay invested even when things become difficult. Remember that risk management strategies should be personalized to your own financial circumstances, goals and risk tolerance. Adapting these strategies to shifting market situations is also crucial. And, as I always say, manage risk first, and P&L second.

1. Diversification

Spreading assets across several classes (stocks, bonds, commodities) and industries might assist in lessening market volatility. Diversification can help to lessen the danger of being too exposed to a particular stock or industry.

I'm not a huge fan of diversification, because I like to take concentrated bets, so this may not be for everyone, but it's certainly a way of reducing your portfolio's volatility. It essentially takes away the concentrated risk that I quite like, so you can see why this may be for some and not others.

It will also help with market fluctuations moving your companies and provide longer-term stability for your returns.

2. Keeping High-Quality Investments

Look for companies that have good fundamentals, steady profit growth, and a track record of weathering economic downturns. Quality businesses are more likely to weather market downturns. Maybe shave or sell your riskier speculative investments. These are the ones that get hammered in a downturn.

There is a natural hedging approach in the stock market since quality investments frequently exhibit features that can assist in offsetting losses and give some protection during market downturns. Here's why retaining great investments can serve as a sort of hedging.

Also, this can be a viable solution to your psychological state. Keeping solid investments in place during market downturns can provide emotional comfort. Knowing they have assets with a higher chance of recovering can limit the desire to make rash selling decisions.

3. Inflation-Resistant Investments

Inflation-resistant investments are those that hold or rise in value during periods of inflation. Investors seek these assets to help safeguard their purchasing power when prices for goods and services rise.

Consider allocating a portion of your portfolio to assets like Treasury Inflation-Protected Bonds (TIPS), real estate, or commodities like gold, which historically have shown resilience during inflationary periods.

4. Regular Rebalancing

Rebalance your portfolio on a regular basis to preserve your desired asset allocation. Rebalancing entails selling some assets that have outperformed others that have underperformed, ensuring that your portfolio remains aligned with your risk tolerance.

One thing a lot of investors get wrong is they have one big position. If that turns the other way, you can see your whole portfolio wiped out very quickly. Make even bets. In the long term, you give yourself a better chance.

5. Assess Your Portfolio's Risk Tolerance

Alter it based on your financial goals and changing market conditions. A portfolio that matches your risk tolerance can help you stay invested even when circumstances are tough.

Keep in mind that individual risk management should be tailored to your own financial situation, goals and risk tolerance. It is also very important to adapt these methods to changing market conditions. Again, manage risk first, not P&L.

6. Staying Informed

This seems obvious, but many investors don't take the time to keep up with news flow in their companies. I mean why wouldn't you? The way I do it is to create my portfolio on several apps and set up an email address for alerts. I check this regularly to see the news.

I also know exactly the timeline of my companies and what events are happening in the future. These are put into a separate calendar. Staying on top of company-specific news is a better use of your time than listening to macro nonsense full of opinions.

Listening to earnings calls, signing up for emails from your companies and joining market forums, as well as social media, are all practical ways to stay informed – however, just ensure these latter ways don't eat up your time. That's the most precious commodity, of course.

7. Fixed Income Allocation

In times of market volatility or uncertainty, increasing your allocation to bonds or other fixed-income assets can provide stability to your portfolio as they tend to be less volatile than stocks. Bonds, for example, are generally thought to be more stable than stocks. This is why boosting your fixed income portfolio can be beneficial during market turbulence. Personally, I am not a fan of bonds but, again, it comes down to risk preference.

8. Hedging with Options

I often hear investors hedging with options and futures. This strategy is another double-edged sword, and if used incorrectly, can lose you more money than you save. I'd say be very familiar with the ways that these complicated instruments work before you use them. They are highly leveraged instruments.

Options methods are regarded as credible stock hedging strategies because they provide investors with a flexible and customizable solution to manage risk. Options are derivative contracts that provide you with the right, but not the responsibility, to buy or sell an underlying asset (such as stocks) at a fixed price (strike price) within a certain time frame.

I have a background in derivatives and, to be honest, I have seen a lot of money lost with investors who don't understand their complexities.

9. Stress Testing

Evaluate how your portfolio would perform under various market scenarios. This can help you identify potential vulnerabilities and adjust your strategy accordingly.

Investors might benefit from stress testing their equity portfolios to see how their investments will fare in severe market situations. It entails modeling severe scenarios and market shocks to assess the potential impact on the value and risk exposure of your portfolio. This is quite a big feat for a newbie, but you'll be surprised at how it opens your eyes to potential risks.

10. Long-Term Perspective

Having a long-term perspective on the stock market for investments is important for several reasons and can quite frankly help with all we have just covered. The important thing is not to use a company's fundamentals moving adversely against you to justify being a "long-term investor".

Long-term investors are willing to invest for at least five years, and preferably ten years or more. They are not concerned with short-term market swings and expect that the stock market will trend upwards over time. Historically, this has been the case.

Being a long-term investor has several advantages. For starters, you are more likely to weather market downturns. The stock market is cyclical, meaning that it will rise and fall over time.

Short-term investors are more inclined to sell their investments while the market is down, missing out on the return. We saw this in heavy collapses in the market, such as the dotcom devastation in 2000 or the housing crisis of 2008. Investors threw the towel in and missed out on a substantial rebound.

Long-term investors, on the other hand, are more likely to stay involved during downturns, and their investments will eventually recover.

Second, compounding benefits long-term investors. The technique of gaining interest on interest is known as compounding. This means your investment will grow more quickly over time. For example, if you invest $100 and get 10% interest each year, you'll end up with $110 at the end of the year. If you leave your money invested for another year, you will earn interest on both the original $100 and the prior year's interest. This means that your investment will be worth $121 dollars at the end of the second year. Compounding can have a significant impact on the long-term growth of your investment.

Third, long-term holders prefer to invest in companies that have significant growth prospects. Short-term investors are more prone to following trends and may invest in businesses that are not long-term viable. Longer-term investors, on the other hand, have the time to investigate companies and invest in those that have a demonstrated track record of profitability and growth.

While this perspective has many advantages, it is critical to assess your investment portfolio on a regular basis to verify that it is still aligned with your goals and risk tolerance.

Finally, whatever stock you buy, act and think like an owner of the business. You'll have a much better perspective for investing, greater confidence and, ultimately, higher returns.

CHAPTER 13

The Psychology of Investing

- How The Financial Brain Works
- The Psychology of the Stock Market
- Why We Lose
- Psychological Traps You Should Avoid
- Logical Vs Illogical
- Be Contrarian to Win

How the Financial Brain Works

"THE MAJORITY IS always wrong; the minority is rarely right" – a lasting quote from Norwegian playwright Henrik Ibsen and a concept I very much buy into. It's much like the Pareto principle, also known as the 80/20 rule, which states that roughly 80% of the effects come from 20% of the causes.

This principle frequently serves as a benchmark for planning, prioritization, and decision making. Individuals and organizations can make more informed and effective decisions and concentrate their efforts in the areas that are most likely to result in meaningful results by identifying the primary elements that account for most of the outcomes.

I apply this principle to most of my life, sometimes unsuccessfully, but when I do, I become much more efficient and productive. I also apply this to investing.

Of course, I analyze the numbers and projections, and most, like me, can do that to a certain extent. However, what I have found over the years is that having an analytical edge isn't enough. The market environment, technology, social media, and the availability of systems that know how companies are performing in real time put us all at a disadvantage.

As well as this, focusing on the behavioral aspect of the investment is just as important as analytics, if not more. Concentrating on this area at the very least can limit your losses.

Do you consider yourself to be a sane investor? Most individuals do. However, we are all emotional creatures. We frequently make fast, stupid decisions due to our thinking, which results in subpar performance or losses.

Surprisingly, most people are correct in their investment decisions, but timing, market movement, fear and greed can ruin potential positive return. Frequently, it comes down to emotion. Investors tend to lose not because of economic conditions, but because of human psychology.

Although some people experience enormous stress because of money worries and the fear of losing their fortune, it is not true to say that this is the greatest worry that all people experience.

Fear is a complex emotion that can vary greatly depending on factors such as environment, culture and prior experience. Many peoples' fear of losing money may be rooted in their sense of insecurity and belief that doing so could lead to undesirable outcomes, be it poverty or social exclusion. However, other phobias can be equally strong and widespread, such as the fear of failure, public speaking, or even death.

Additionally, it's critical to keep in mind that a person's level of financial stress can vary significantly depending on their individual circumstances, including their financial situation, stage of life, and personal priorities. For instance, someone who has gone through a severe financial struggle may be more afraid of losing money than someone who has not experienced such difficulties.

Attention, perception, memory, and decision making are just a few of the cognitive processes that the brain uses when processing financial data. The brain engages neural circuits that assist in processing and analyzing financial information. For instance, the prefrontal cortex, a region of the brain in charge of executive function, attention, and decision making, is strongly engaged while making financial decisions.

When people suffer financial stress or anxiety, the amygdala, a region of the brain responsible for processing emotions, is also triggered. Additionally, the brain's reward system, which dopamine activates, influences how we make financial decisions. When people receive money or experience financial gains, the brain releases dopamine, which gives them a sense of pleasure and reward.

In brief conclusion, it is not true to suggest that the greatest fear of all humans is money, even though it can be a substantial source of worry and anxiety for some. People's unique experiences and circumstances can affect their fears and priorities, because fear is a complicated emotion influenced by many variables.

The Psychology of the Stock Market

The psychology of the market refers to the role that human behavior and emotions play in shaping market trends and investor decision making.

Everything in the world moves in cycles: seasonal cycles, ecological cycles, geological cycles, technological cycles, economic cycles, and even smaller cycles such as relationship cycles. Did you feel like things started to get better after that huge argument with your partner? No? Give it time; it will.

Companies and markets fluctuate with economics, performance and investor sentiment. My view is that everything will have value in the long term. The trouble is, in the gap between investing at the price and the goal of realizing a return on your investment, many shorter-term influences can get in the way and cause you losses. Being able to recognize these cycles and emotional influences will get you up there with the greats and away from the masses. The analytical part is easy.

As the legendary investor Benjamin Graham states, "In the short run, the market is a voting machine, but in the long run, it is a weighing machine."

Why We Lose

In my 30-plus years in the market, I have seen many cycles, bubbles and downturns. My tested emotional intelligence (EI) score is off the charts, so I have the uncanny ability to notice and process more than most, particularly in terms of people, and the way they are likely to think due to their personalities as well as reactions to different situations, something I believe I inherited from my mom.

As money is the sole driver in stock markets, it becomes a magnifying glass of reactions and emotions when events happen. It's here, at extremes, where I consider myself to be at my best. My contrarian brain kicks in, and I spot investment opportunities. I have made my greatest investments with a contrarian lens.

I've seen fortunes made and fortunes lost throughout the years. Nothing, however, replaces consistency and hard work in maintaining your wealth. There are no get rich quick schemes.

The dot-com era in 2000 was one of the most incredible experiences of my life so far. The fast rise in technology shares made millionaires overnight but also increased deception and fraud as the lust for greed increased.

The collapse was something else. Stocks that went from nothing to some of the biggest companies in the world, such as Juniper Networks (JNPR), reaching such heady heights and then almost returning to dust within a year, were incredible to watch. Around 90% of dot-com stocks in that era went to zero, along with the profits of many investors.

Individuals frequently act irrationally and exhibit a wide range of reactions. For instance, many investors made large investments in internet-related stocks during the dot-com boom. However, many of these stocks lost value when the bubble burst, and many investors suffered sizable losses.

The fear in 2001/2 was some of the greatest I've seen in markets. It took 12 years after that for the S&P to reach its previous high. Investors went into what is known as the irrational exuberance trap, which essentially means that unfounded market optimism lacks a real foundation of fundamental valuation, but instead rests on psychological factors.

Remember, some of the worst losses in the stock market come naturally, from buying stocks that are too highly priced. The surprising fact is that investors buy stocks knowing full well that they are overpriced but expecting to sell them to someone else at an even higher price.

Their perception is based on the underlying "Greater Fool Theory", which simply states that there will always be a "greater fool" in the market who will be ready to pay a price based on a higher valuation for an already overvalued asset.

This is a huge gamble for investors and not one I recommend placing your hard-earned cash on, but it is a very common strategy for foolish investors that comes with irrational exuberance.

Investors' emotions swing wildly from optimism to pessimism, from greed to terror, from credulity to skepticism, and from risk tolerance to risk aversion.

One memory stands out very clearly: when I visited a tech firm whose share price was on an incredible vertical move, the secretary was flicking through a Ferrari magazine. That characterized a lot of that period for me. It's not that I'm against well-paid secretaries, it was just an anomaly I wasn't used to seeing. The truth about markets is that they are made up of people who come with all those human emotions, fears and propensities for extremes.

What you must remember is that, on the face of it, no one loses in the stock market, and of course everyone wins. It's like social media. When did you last put a photo up of your beat-up old car or a selfie in the morning after a rough night, other than for a joke? Never, of course. You want to show everyone that you are winning. The reality is that only a select few win long term – the 20%.

That desire to win or show you are winning, or more importantly, not losing, can make you do things you wouldn't normally do. Perhaps buy that new, exuberant car above your means or pay for extensive cosmetic surgery on credit that you may struggle to re-pay.

None of this is wrong, but understanding why you are doing it really matters. It's the same for investing. No one wants to lose, so if emotion instead of analysis drives your pursuit of these things, you might find that you lose more than you win. It's this very emotion that leads us to sing about small profits and keep quiet about large losses. Our vanity matters to the world.

If you remember one thing, remember this. The markets were set up to fool you. They are there to take your money. Contrary to popular belief, you will never teach the market any sort of lesson. You must try to outsmart it, but that's easier said than done.

Psychological Traps You Should Avoid

The "behavioral" edge I often speak about can come in many forms. Just to clarify, your behavioral edge is one of two things that are essential for investing. The first is your analytical edge, which encompasses the numbers, and the second is your "behavioral" edge, which we discussed in Chapter 10.

It's also important to ensure you don't influence that behavioral edge with your own cognitive biases. The tendency of the human brain to streamline information processing through a filter of personal experience and preferences results in cognitive bias, which is a systematic thought process.

It's something that could mean the difference between a good or bad investment if you don't control it. The list of biases is extensive and serves as a good guideline to ensure you are less influenced by your brain's emotions and influenced by the facts as much as possible.

In 2020 and through 2021, the world was exceptionally socially bored. We were in the middle of the Covid pandemic. There was no traveling, no sports, activity was restricted, and the mental health and wellbeing of the public were raising concerns.

People were frustrated and spent their money on new motor vehicles, recreational goods, furniture, appliances, and pets. All fueled by government stimulus checks and low-cost or free loans.

The absence of live sports betting caused the smaller investor to turn his attention to the stock market, as my good friend Spencer Jakab points out in his must-read book, *The Revolution That Wasn't: GameStop, Reddit, and the Fleecing of Small Investors*: "Disrespect for traditional expertise was a driving factor at the time. People like Warren Buffett were cautious at the pandemic's onset, but brand-new influencers with no track record who used social media (Twitter, TikTok and YouTube) weren't. Their advice turned out to be right, given the eventual return to normal and the incredible burst of fiscal and monetary stimulus." He was correct, and it snowballed into a huge, popular stock rally in 2021, officially known as the "meme rally".

Back to psychology: confirmation bias is a cognitive bias that is seen in every area of life and can be obvious in the stock market.

When people look for information or proof that supports their previous views or hypotheses while ignoring information that contradicts them, this is known as the "confirmation trap". You see it all the time, particularly on social media. On Twitter or Facebook, for example, you are likely to surround yourself with like-minded friends.

Really, this serves no purpose other than to bolster your beliefs and, in some cases, your ego too. The truth can be far from what you and your group believe, as it chooses not to listen to anything else.

With investing, we saw a lot of this in the meme craze. Shares of companies that went viral due to a heightened social mood were referred to as "meme stocks".

AMC and GameStop saw huge increases in their stock values. There were a lot of news stories about people raising the share prices that were not particularly profitable in general. Peloton (PTON), Zoom (ZM), Bed Bath & Beyond (BBBY), and even Blackberry (BB) were companies that achieved lofty values that weren't really justified by their balance sheets, but investors, mainly the new and smaller ones, continued to purchase because they were convinced there was an upside.

Their knowledge came from online sources such as "Wallstreetbets" (WSB), a subreddit where participants discuss stock and option trading and used to gather in their thousands every morning. These investors would seek out stories and testimonials that supported their beliefs while ignoring or dismissing fundamental evidence that contradicted them.

What was interesting to me was that the bias gained momentum and, by the end, it was difficult to know what was and wasn't a "meme" stock. All stocks were popular. If you owned one beforehand, consider yourself a lucky investor, as the price was catapulted higher for no apparent reason other than that it appeared to gain popularity suddenly.

Looking back at the bubble, it's an important lesson and a reason to examine what happened. Investors who held on to most of these names suddenly found themselves underwater.

A combination of regulatory, market and social factors contributed to the end of the meme stock phase. Regulatory agencies, including the Securities and Exchange Commission (SEC), started looking into possible market manipulation and other abuses related to social media-driven trading activity as meme stocks became more and more popular.

Additionally, some social media platforms and online forums started to restrict conversations about meme stocks, which might have lessened their appeal to some investors, and the subsequent downturn left a lot of them feeling that their emotional investment in these stocks, which weren't worth anything like what they paid for them, prevented them from taking a loss.

It's vanity, as I mentioned earlier, that is one of the single greatest enemies to stock market success, and confirmation bias, along with vanity, proved deadly. The collapse in meme names contributed, in 2022, to the stock market's worst fall since 2008.

This leads to the sunk cost trap. This bias happens when people keep devoting time, money or other resources to a project just because they have already devoted so much of these resources to the project.

This bias may influence individuals' judgment and result in the wasteful use of resources. This happens frequently when investors buy a stock and, subsequently, the stock falls, and they feel like they must keep averaging because they have put "good money" in already.

This is a real path to loss for investors. Maintaining disciplined stop losses based on your risk criteria and being prepared to exit losing investments when necessary, instead of holding onto them indefinitely, will support this goal.

We saw evidence of this playing out when the market reached its peak in December 2021. For many investors the following year was a rude awakening in their own convictions. Their sunken cost had already pushed their average down, particularly on some of the meme names that fell very fast and ultimately ended in disaster as it dawned on them that price didn't equal valuation and momentum was the only thing that was holding them up when the music stopped.

A lot of the meme phase was also based on the anchoring trap. This happens when someone bases too much of their decision or judgment on the first piece of information they are presented with.

This can happen frequently to many investors as they go looking for something, find it and act upon it without looking further. In the case of stocks, you might be looking for a cheap small-cap company in the industrials sector and stumble upon one that fits the bill, even though there could be multiple companies in the sector.

To avoid falling into the anchoring trap, it is important to gather multiple sources of information, consider all relevant factors before deciding, and try to challenge your original thinking. Producing a relative value table will ensure you capture some of the chosen companies' competitors, and carrying out further analysis may lead you to a better choice of investment.

This trap can take many forms, and one of the more obvious ones is "buy" or "sell" levels. How often have you heard "$100 is the buy level" or "$200 is the sell". Buyers and sellers are fixed or "anchored" to these prices. They will psychologically obsess on that price when determining when to buy or sell more of the same stock, regardless of the stock's true value as determined by an evaluation of pertinent aspects or fundamentals affecting it.

It is important to take a broader view of the situation and to consider a range of factors, such as market trends, company performance and economic conditions, to avoid doing this.

Social Media

Have you ever noticed that some social media accounts just rely on the past for their assumptions and analysis? The relativity trap is a classic cognitive bias people bring to markets and investing. Instead of making an unbiased evaluation of the event itself, investors tend to assess the seriousness of a problem or scenario by comparing it to others.

Personally, I never buy into this thinking, although the number of times I hear it is incredible. Macro guys are often the perpetrators of this type of bias.

My experience leads me to believe that history does indeed repeat itself. Bubbles, manias and crashes ultimately have the same effect, ending in loss of wealth. However, here is the key difference: they come in different disguises. From what I recall, the market has never reached its peak or bottom in the same scenario. It just doesn't happen. Fear and greed are what happened, and these two traits are the same at both ends of the market, and they do indeed repeat.

It is crucial to assess issues and circumstances on their own merits, rather than in comparison to others, to avoid falling into the relativity trap. In addition, rather than becoming bogged down in comparisons to others, it can be beneficial to concentrate on solutions and actions that can be taken to solve the situation. Lastly, try to ignore social media that purports this sort of analysis. It can have a heavy influence.

Logical vs Illogical

We live in a world today where illogical behavior can seem a bit smarter than logical behavior. Take Warren Buffett, for example. It's obvious what he does. He even goes so far as to say what companies he looks for. He weeds out companies that appear to be trading below their true worth. He says that there isn't a single way to measure value. Businesses with long-term earning potential typically have steady profits, positive cash flow and little debt. How easy is that?

With this simple strategy and a bit of patience, he has become one of the best investors in the world. I mean, you can even copy his portfolio.

Why do investors often engage in unethical actions driven by irrational behavior? The perception is that the chances of success are greatly enhanced by doing what seems illogical these days. You see this a lot on social media.

Take the dislike of Elon Musk, Jeff Bezos and Mark Zuckerberg. Though they have produced some of the most successful firms in the world, they still deal with a lot of people who oppose them or their businesses, usually citing baseless claims of fraud as the basis behind their disdain.

Although some investors might gamble on the share price declining based on this negativity as information, this thinking is illogical.

The pseudo-certainty trap is along similar lines and is one that many stubborn portfolio managers fall into. They tend to be extremely certain and reluctant to change their opinions because they are overconfident in their own judgments and ideas.

This also encompasses the blindness trap, also known as the "blind spot bias" – a cognitive bias in which people tend to believe that they are more objective and rational than other people and are unconscious of their own biases. This can impair their capacity to assess information and come to wise conclusions, as well as cause them to fail to understand their own limitations.

It's always good to get a second or alternative opinion on major decisions. The least you'll do is ensure you are making a rational judgment.

Be Contrarian to Win

One of my greatest pieces of advice is try your best to stay humble – otherwise, the market will take it upon itself to humble you.

Lastly, maintaining a healthy skepticism and carefully weighing the risks and possible rewards of any investment or market are crucial for avoiding psychological traps.

Do your research, keep it current, always keep your eyes forward and never look back.

Assuming the masses will fall into the traps covered in the section, the way to win at investing is to do exactly the opposite of what nearly everyone else is doing.

CHAPTER 14

Wealth Can Be Created on the Way Down in the Stock Market – It's Just Not Obvious

- → The Pump & Dump
- → Historical Perspective
- → How to Position Yourself
- → Three Things to Help You Increase Your Wealth

WARREN BUFFETT'S RIGHT-HAND man, the late Charlie Munger, once said, "If you're going to invest in stocks for the longer term, there are going to be periods when there's a lot of agony. I think you just have to learn to live through them."

The Pump and Dump

At the time of writing in 2023, the last ten months have been very rough, to say the least, if you are a stock investor. The S&P 500 Index is down 22% year to date, but that isn't representative of the base of the 24 million new investors that have come to the market in the last two years.

Many popularly held stocks are down a great deal more, and the technology sector has been decimated. Investors have been heavily selling off growth businesses on the theory that companies that performed best during boom times will be disproportionately affected by the rising interest rates and inflation we are now enduring.

The NASDAQ is down 30% year to date. We are having a very serious correction after the economy was pumped with trillions of dollars of stimulus checks and other monetary aid.

These stimulus checks were responsible for opening a host of brand-new Robinhood trading accounts from mainly furloughed individuals, who were unable to bet elsewhere (such as sports), which in turn propelled the stock market to all-time highs and pushed the S&P 500 to a huge 27% gain in 2021.

Sadly, the rally looked like it had as much substance as cotton candy and is now disappearing. So the fun times are over. Those days of watching stocks go up with quick profits are gone for the foreseeable future, it appears.

With some of the most darling popular (meme) companies at the time losing between 50% and 70%, and in some cases, like Peloton Interactive, Inc. (PTON), losing over 90% of its value, this has forced some investors to either throw in the towel or turn into unwilling "long-term investors" with companies that may never see the light of day again. Refer to the fallout from the 2000 collapse.

Historical Perspective

So, what should you do now? Before we get there, let's look at what is going on and try to put a little perspective behind it.

A good index full of quality companies will go up over time, because quality companies simply grow. The problem is that growth does not always happen in a straight line. I've been around nearly 35 years in this space and if you are a novice, you'll soon learn that quality equity indices are likely to maintain a long-term rising trend with just small breaks between the larger cycles.

Let's assume we are speaking about the S&P 500, a stock market index tracking the performance of 500 large companies listed on stock exchanges in the United States. It is one of the most followed equity indices, with some of the best companies in the world as constituents.

According to what we are hearing from the media, the world economy is in a mess. You may be hearing all the bad news now and wondering why you are even invested in stocks. I would tend to agree with you.

Losing money is extremely hard to justify in any scenario, but hold on a minute. The chart below shows the performance of the index since the infamous 1929 crash. There were plenty of "bad" events during the journey up until now, but on a longer-term scale, they really didn't even register, and buying every dip resulted in some great gains if you had the stomach to act upon it.

As an investor, you must also be aware that the market will

occasionally decline. You shouldn't own stocks if you're not prepared for this. And when it occurs, it's a positive.

"There will be bear markets about twice every ten years and recessions about twice every ten or 12 years, but nobody has been able to predict them reliably," said investor John Templeton. "So the best thing to do is to buy when shares are thoroughly depressed and that means when other people are selling."

He's been correct, and there is no reason to think any differently going forward. The trick is to take out the emotion when the media (and sometimes your close friends) are full of doom and gloom. Easier said than done, I know.

Inflation and S&P 500, 1929 to 2021

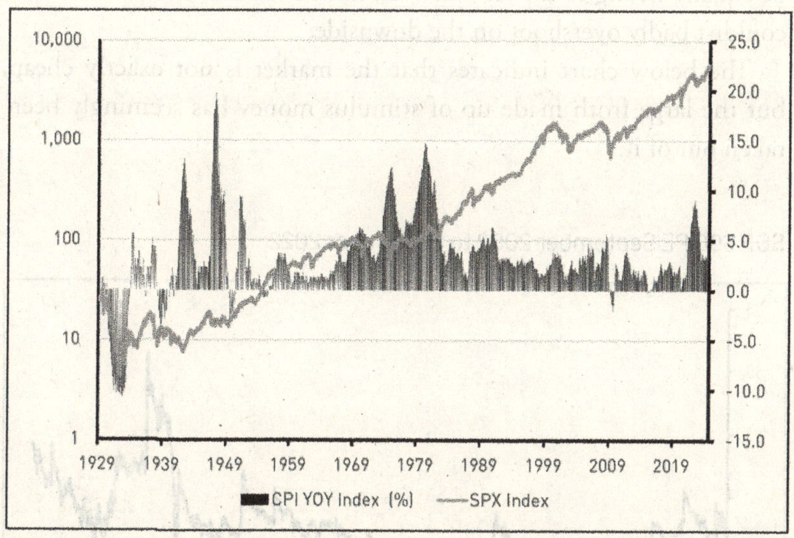

S&P 500 vs Inflation with Historical Events

Let's look at another metric that puts the pullback of the market into perspective: the price-to-earnings ratio of the S&P 500.

A P/E is calculated by dividing the stock's current price by its latest earnings per share. A high P/E ratio for a company suggests that investors see it as a growth stock. It may also mean that the stock is overvalued. From an index perspective, we look to be somewhere in the middle of the range, judging by the last 20 years.

Things may seem bad now, and perpetual bears would try to convince you that the world is ending, but expecting every bad market to result in the Great Depression would be absurd. It would be equally wrong to expect that a fall from overvalued to more valued couldn't badly overshoot on the downside.

The below chart indicates that the market is not exactly cheap, but the large froth made up of stimulus money has seemingly been taken out of it.

S&P 500 PE September 2002 to September 2022

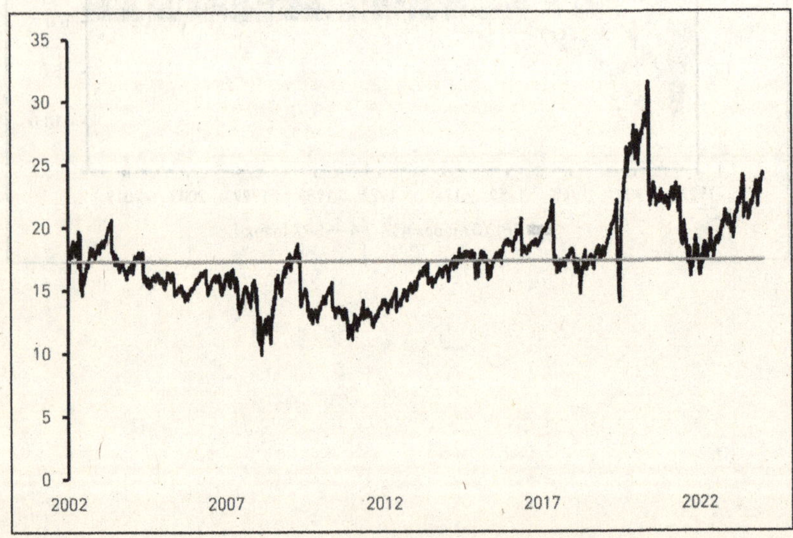

S&P Large Cap Price Earnings Ratio

I'm not a huge fan of macro data overall, because it is usually unactionable and very subjective, but the recent pump and dump was a global phenomenon. The fallout is persistent inflation, hawkish governments, lower GDP and slowing economies.

We have the odd situation that the whole world is suffering from the same scenario due to the pandemic. With this overshadowing everything, you can bet that it will take a long while to unwind the mess, and the turnaround could be "another while" after that.

Ask yourself, what will change the economy and move the market back up? The US stock market did not fully recover from the fall 2008 stock market meltdown until mid-2013. To put the move in perspective, it should be noted that the S&P 500 needed over 12 years to break and maintain the highs reached during the tech boom in 2000.

How to Position Yourself

I often say, "buy companies, not markets", and I truly believe you can perform by buying good-quality businesses and investing like an owner without having to think about what the stock market is doing.

Predicting markets is a fool's game, and direction will play on your emotion. Every commentator now is full of bad news, and never forget that bad news sells. It can be very challenging to think differently when the audience is essentially unified in its sentiments and decisions.

Think contrarian when the overwhelming feeling is going one way. Predicting wider markets will also whip you around all over the place. To be honest, your stock picks shouldn't really depend on the market direction if you are a true long-term value investor.

The likelihood that you will make a poor decision increases as you make more decisions with investments. Do your homework. Be very selective, be small and ready to manage in a volatile market, and always start by analyzing the risk *first*. You'll be part of the elite if you do this.

The stock market was set up to fool you, not to make you money. Start with this statement every time you analyze an investment; it will help enormously with discounting the emotional element that can so often be attributed to losses.

Three Things to Help You Increase Your Future Wealth

Let's assume that market prices are "fair" (debatable, I know). Let's also assume that the economy will take a while to turn around. What can you do to take advantage of the situation and boost your wealth down the line?

First, always examine and outline what you are looking to achieve from investing. It is crucial for an investor to question, "What is my objective?" before buying any stocks when designing an investing program.

In my experience, people generally want a retirement program, and look for good-quality companies to invest in along the way to keep it interesting; but ensure you discuss this with your financial advisor before you act, and never invest more than you are prepared to lose.

Second, invest in a good-quality index. The practice of investing a set dollar amount on a regular basis (usually monthly), independent of the index price, is known as "dollar cost averaging". It's a terrific method to form a disciplined investing habit, increase your investment efficiency, and possibly reduce your stress, as well as your expenses. Never underestimate the ability to have a good night's sleep.

The rub of this strategy, particularly at the current time, is that you may wait a long while for returns to come through. Sometimes you may see a reduction in wealth before it increases, and you may become agitated and bored.

If you stick to the playbook, the longer term should see substantial gains. No one predicts the market with any sort of consistency, but this way you don't need a view. You are betting on the longer-term trend, which we have seen followed.

Thirdly, invest in companies that have a catalyst event that will potentially move the price to value. As an individual investor or even a private investor, I am amazed that I still see people over-analyze the same old stocks.

As we have seen, stocks can stay cheap for years and, in my experience, great opportunities are to be found in the places that have been neglected and where other people are not looking. Especially in these sorts of markets where the most popular companies are under so much scrutiny. Where is your edge above and beyond the wider market in your chosen investment? Everything is "cheap", but what will move it?

Find stock with a catalyst (or situation) to propel it to a higher value. Seek out events that are not widely advertised: spin-offs, split-offs, Reverse Morris Trusts, squeeze-outs, deeply discounted rights offerings, changes of management, insider buying by good management, restructurings, and companies emerging from bankruptcy. This is the pond where you should cast your net and fish. These "special situations" are proven areas of success if analyzed correctly.

For example, spin-offs have been proven to outperform the market by 10% each year for the last 20 years. We at The Edge look specifically at these catalyst events and help investors large and small find and analyze the best opportunities from a value creation perspective.

Value investing is practically alone among techniques that provide you exposure to the upside with minimal downside risk, so in a bear market that discipline becomes crucial.

Add in a catalyst event and you are set up for an extremely powerful potential return if you have carried out your homework correctly. If you're investing with a long-time horizon, having an equity bias makes sense; stocks go up in the long run.

CHAPTER 15

Financial Risks: How Stock Market Predictions Lead to Losses

- Complexity Of Market Dynamics
- Information Overload
- Emotional And Psychological Factors
- External Factors and Their Unpredictability
- Limitations Of Predictive Models
- Conclusion

THE PURSUIT OF market predictions by investors becomes risky given the potential for a single tweet to cause a stock market avalanche. As they traverse an intricate network of economic information, psychological prejudices, and unanticipated worldwide events, the consequences are frequently severe, and the stakes are impossibly high.

Investors who acknowledge these challenges often mitigate risk through a range of strategies, such as diversification, hedging, and continuous monitoring of market conditions and assumptions. The inherent uncertainty in markets means that even with sophisticated models and deep experience, predictions are often just educated guesses.

I am an individual company investor. I invest in the future outcomes of the company and rarely, if ever, do macro-economic conditions and numbers come into play in my analysis. I don't invest in biotech, and I don't invest in commodities.

Notable financial institutions such as Morgan Stanley, J.P. Morgan, and BlackRock have issued recent market forecasts for 2024 that reflect worries about valuation, economic growth, and possible geopolitical dangers. While J.P. Morgan projects little earnings growth and highlights the effect of recalcitrant inflation on interest rates, Morgan Stanley cautions against overvalued stocks and too-rosy corporate earnings projections. BlackRock recommends keeping a balanced and diversified investing approach even if it finds chances for active management in the face of market dispersion.

These studies emphasize the difficulties in precisely forecasting market trends in a complicated and unpredictable international setting.

Complexity of Market Dynamics

It is essential for seasoned investors to know how various elements interact to drive market dynamics. Many factors have a big impact on market mood and results, including political events, economic indicators, and company activities. Fundamental economic indicators include employment numbers, GDP growth rates, and inflation figures.

Usually, optimistic market data sparks rallies. If the same statistics raise worries about inflation and ensuing central bank interest rate increases, it can nevertheless cause market volatility.

Political events that play significant roles include elections, policy changes, and geopolitical developments. The anticipation of regulatory changes, for instance, can cause market anxiety, even though it might also help the market rise. These incidents can have a big and instantaneous effect, which shows how sensitive markets are to political stability and government acts.

Corporate actions can have an impact on the market at large as well as immediately affecting the stock prices of the companies concerned. Examples of these decisions are earnings reports, mergers, and leadership changes. Sector revaluations may result from strategic business mergers, although poor performance by a top company can also lower the sector.

Unexpected actions in the market may result from the convergence of these elements. The cumulative effects of several dynamics are what markets react to, not to any one element acting alone. Complex market reactions might arise from this interaction when political instability, for instance, obscures strong economic signals or vice versa.

Successfully navigating the markets requires an understanding of their intricacy. Understanding the relationships and effects between these factors facilitates the creation of a sophisticated investment plan that considers the inherent volatility of the markets as well as the predictable trends. Long-term investing success requires this comprehensive approach.

Information Overload

Investors are inundated with a ton of data in today's digital era, from news stories, market reports, economic indicators, and social media feeds. Though it may appear helpful, having so much information can make decision making more difficult and result in information overload.

The main difficulty is sorting through this information to determine what is important for making wise financial choices. Information is not equal; certain data can significantly influence market changes, while others are just noise that may confuse or divert attention.

Important economic announcements, such as changes in interest rates or unemployment statistics, can direct investment plans, for instance. Sensational news headlines, however, can elicit strong market responses right away but frequently have little lasting impact.

Investors need to have strong analytical abilities and instruments to sift through the deluge of information and concentrate on what is important. The challenge lies in the variety and speed of the information, as well as its amount. Rapid updating of the information frequently results in contradictory interpretations that impair judgment.

Emotional and Psychological Factors

Experienced investors frequently control this overload with AI, computerized trading algorithms, and sophisticated data analytics. By sifting through huge databases, these tools can help extract useful insights and spot less obvious underlying trends. Still, a big problem is the possibility of analysis paralysis, in which an excess of data prevents decision making.

In the end, wise discernment of the caliber and applicability of the information is just as important for successful investing in the current climate. In the choppy world of finance, keeping a clear perspective requires striking a balance between being knowledgeable and being overwhelmed.

Not only do market movements and numerical data form the world of investing, but the psychological composition of the investors themselves has a big impact. Cognitive biases, especially confirmation bias and overconfidence, are important in influencing financial decisions, and they frequently result in worse than ideal results.

Confidence is too high when investors place unduly strong trust in their own instincts or analytical abilities, resulting in biased results. Investors who suffer from this prejudice overestimate the precision of their forecasts and underestimate the dangers.

For example, an overly confident investor could disregard warning indicators of a downturn because they are so confident in their chosen approach or in their previous success, which they credit too much to their own abilities rather than to chance or market conditions.

Investors who have confirmation bias look for or value information that supports their pre-existing ideas or theories more highly than information that might challenge them. This can create a risky loop, whereby an investor sticks with a failing investment because of the biased information that backs up their original choice instead of reassessing their position and considering a more nuanced analysis of fresh information.

These prejudices cause erroneous thinking and, eventually, investment decisions that do not correspond with impartial evaluations of risk and reward, therefore compromising decision making. Frequently, the outcome is a confirmation of false beliefs and a rise in investing mistakes, such as hanging onto losing positions too long or placing unduly large wagers on speculative results.

Investors hoping to make reasonable, well-informed judgments must recognize and lessen the impact of these psychological biases. Methods for overcoming these prejudices include looking for different viewpoints, methodically analyzing contradicting data, and establishing preset guidelines for financial decisions.

CHAPTER 15

External Factors and their Unpredictability

Investing is frequently surrounded by uncertainties arising from outside variables that are hard to forecast and model. There are a few things that quickly and dramatically impact the investing environment, such as geopolitical tensions, natural disasters, and unforeseen regulatory changes.

Global financial markets can be volatile due to geopolitical tensions, including wars, trade conflicts, and political change and upheaval. Trade tariffs, for instance, have the potential to upset international supply networks and lower corporate profitability all around. Similar swings in commodity prices, such as oil, or the quick devaluation of currencies can result from political unrest.

Natural disasters provide other formidable obstacles. Because they wreck so much, earthquakes, hurricanes, and other calamities can cause insurance firms to lose a lot of money, severely disrupt supply networks, and lower consumer spending. These occurrences are extremely difficult to model in investment strategies because of their unpredictable timing and impact.

Shocks from without can upset the rational conduct and market efficiency that are common assumptions in traditional financial models. Since unusual and unprecedented events lack previous data, these models are useless for predicting these events. Usually, these models use historical data to forecast future trends.

It is also difficult to forecast market reactions because of the interdependence of global markets, which allows an incident in one region of the world to have repercussions elsewhere. A large commodity-exporting nation's political change, for example, can have an impact on commodity prices globally, which in turn affects businesses and economies everywhere.

Managing these difficulties calls for investors to maintain flexibility in their approaches and to keep an eye on a broad spectrum of possible risk variables. To reduce the risks connected to the unpredictable nature of external events, scenario planning, hedging techniques, and diversification are crucial instruments. These strategies protect investments from sudden market changes brought about by unforeseen circumstances through their preparation for potential outcomes.

Limitations of Predictive Models

Predicting future market behaviors is sometimes quite difficult because of the dependence on prior data and the underlying assumptions of financial models. Although these models are necessary instruments for investors, several important elements can undermine their efficacy.

Financial models often use previous data and assumptions to project future results. This method makes the potentially serious incorrect assumption that relationships and patterns from the past will persist into the future. A complex, dynamic array of factors affects market dynamics. When future conditions differ significantly from the past, depending solely on historical tendencies can result in serious mistakes.

Market structure changes: The financial markets change with time; they are never static. Changes in consumer behavior, regulatory environments, or technological breakthroughs can all affect market structures. Because algorithmic trading has grown, for example, trade volumes and price movements have changed, which affects how predictable stock prices are based on past trends. In the same vein, new financial goods and instruments can bring about behaviors that were not taken into consideration in previous models.

Economic fundamentals: Unexpected variations in interest rates, employment levels, or inflation rates can quickly make current models out of date. Models relying on data from stable economic conditions, for instance, could not be able to forecast market collapses or the actions of investors in panic during times of economic crisis.

Another crucial flaw is the dependence on the presumption that economic links stay the same across time. Variables like unemployment and stock market performance might have different relationships as the economy changes structurally or as new economic policies are implemented.

Investors and analysts must constantly test and update their models against current data to reduce these risks, and they must also be wary of the limitations of any model-based forecast. Stress-testing portfolios against unforeseen events and including a variety of scenarios can also help control the risks connected to depending too much on previous data. More accurate forecasts need models to be adjusted to reflect current market conditions rather than presuming historical continuity.

Conclusion

Seeking market forecasts in the ever-changing world of investment is like trying to navigate a maze that is always being renovated; new routes appear and disappear overnight. Macroeconomic changes, unanticipated geopolitical developments, and ingrained psychological prejudices that warp perception and decision-making processes are only a few of the interrelated causes of this complexity.

The difficulties abound. First, investors can experience information overload from the abundance of material available to them, which frequently obscures the important from the insignificant. Business activities, political events, and economic indicators all create a complex tapestry from which it takes keen analytical skills to separate the significant from the insignificant.

Second, the unpredictability of outside factors – whether they be natural disasters or geopolitical tensions – adds levels of complexity to investment strategies and frequently makes conventional models useless. Built on past data, these models find it difficult to keep up with the quick changes in economic foundations and market structures.

According to recent evaluations by renowned companies like Morgan Stanley, J.P. Morgan, and BlackRock, relying solely on forecast models that ignore new, evolving economic realities is risky. These projections emphasize the few growth opportunities in the face of increased prices and emphasize the need for a well-rounded and diverse investment strategy.

It takes recognition of these complex issues together with strong risk management techniques to successfully negotiate this complex investment terrain. Not only strategic decisions but also necessary strategies to reduce possible losses include diversification, ongoing market condition monitoring, and hedging.

Furthermore, the underlying risks of the market require investors to pledge to ongoing education and flexibility to make well-informed and current investing choices. This strategy strengthens the investor's ability to weather the shocks of unanticipated market volatility, in addition to increasing the possibility of obtaining long-term rewards.

CHAPTER 16

How to Lose Money in the Stock Market

- The Stock Market as an Ocean
- The Allure and Illusion of Following Trends
- The Charismatic Leader
- Groupthink
- Herd Mentality
- Emotional Investing
- Be Like Buffett
- Conclusion

MAKING A SMALL fortune is simple – you just start with a large fortune. Sounds absurd, right? This dichotomy, as strange as it sounds, is what propels us into the obscure realm of financial blunders.

You may wonder why it's important to dwell on loss. Our journey today will be unlike any other. We will turn our attention away from the dogged quest for profit and instead master the finer points of financial mismanagement, avoiding traps and learning from our mistakes.

I have been through the ups and downs of the market on many occasions, from busy trading floors to high-stakes boardrooms, over my 30 years as a trader, portfolio manager, investor, and advisor to important decision makers. My life's work has been to unearth hidden company value and to realize it not only for investors and clients, but also for myself.

Nevertheless, we are changing gears today. Our focus here is on personal rebalancing and the art of avoiding financial disaster, rather than asset devaluation. Get ready for an illuminating adventure where the key to safeguarding our fortune is learning to lose intelligently.

The Stock Market as an Ocean

Envision the stock market as an expansive ocean, where the tranquility of calm waters can, without warning, give way to stormy turbulence. This sea of finance pulses with volatility, its currents shaped by the unforeseen – natural disasters, political upheaval, or the latest market whispers – each event sending ripples or formidable tsunamis across the financial landscape.

Even the slightest news can disturb this ocean, be it a minor adjustment in interest rates or a groundbreaking innovation, underscoring the market's acute sensitivity to global happenings, investor sentiment, and the fortunes of companies.

Amid these waves swim the swift currents of high-frequency trading and the rare, unforeseeable "black swan" events, each layer adding complexity and unpredictability.

Yet it is within this very ebb and flow that the greatest opportunities – and the gravest risks – lie. Today, we set sail into the market's rougher tides, delving into how fortunes can swiftly change and, more critically, how to steer through financial storms without foundering. Let us explore three common ways investors lose money, and how understanding these pitfalls can better prepare us for the tumultuous journey ahead.

The Allure and Illusion of Following Trends

In 1841, Charles Mackay wrote one of my favorite all time classic books: *Extraordinary Popular Delusions and the Madness of Crowds*. This book is a journey into the human mind and emotions we all experience, uncovering the roots of mass hysteria. Why do intelligent people fall for absurd beliefs? Through tales of the South Sea Bubble, the Tulip Mania – where flowers were valued above gold – and the Mississippi Scheme, Mackay reveals a pattern of collective folly leading to financial ruin.

History, as he shows, has a habit of repeating itself. We're often fooled, misled, by the very markets we trust. Remember, markets were built on deception, not gain. This is not just history; it's a lesson for today, a warning that the madness of crowds is alive and well, and why you, sitting here, should care.

The Charismatic Leader

In a story straight out of *Extraordinary Popular Delusions and the Madness of Crowds*, we rewind to November 2022 and see the collapse of FTX, a massive cryptocurrency, and its creator, Sam Bankman-Fried. Once heralded as a crypto wunderkind, Bankman-Fried presided over FTX's monumental collapse because of his careless handling of client assets, which caused a panic withdrawal that the platform was unable to withstand. Due to the massive losses suffered by investors and the subsequent damage to the integrity of the cryptocurrency industry, this collapse will go down in history as a dark chapter in financial follies.

Like the timeless cautions expressed in Charles Mackay's work, this tale illustrates how the temptation of large profits and the charisma of an apparently forward-thinking leader may cause even the most astute individuals to lose sight of reality.

The stunning ascent and fall of Bankman-Fried is a sobering reminder that no amount of brainpower can withstand the overwhelming flow of popular illusion. Once again, the craziness of crowds spares no one, as notable personalities and astute investors such as Tom Brady and Softbank were swept up in the frenzy. A cautionary tale for our times, this narrative of a company's decline highlights the ageless validity of Mackay's lessons.

Groupthink

The tragic stories of Wirecard and Luckin Coffee bring groupthink and its financial dangers to life, showcasing a psychological trap that causes even the most intelligent people to commit collective mistakes. After promising a 500% profit gain by 2025, the once-glowing German stock market jewel Wirecard fell abruptly in 2020, with a €1.9 billion hole in its accounting, causing one of the biggest financial crashes in Germany and leading to the CEO's arrest for fraud.

Then there's Luckin Coffee, a Chinese brand that gained traction on NASDAQ as a serious competitor to Starbucks, thanks to its fast expansion and claims of revolutionizing tea culture in China. But in 2020, it came to light that a lot of its sales were fake, which caused a disastrous drop in shares and delisting.

The perils of groupthink in investing are highlighted by these scandals. The attraction of a captivating story and the echo chamber of investor enthusiasm can cause us to miss obvious warning signs. These examples clearly demonstrate the dangers of going along with the crowd and the importance of conducting one's own research.

Herd Mentality

Think about this: In September 2020, a remarkable story comes to light, exemplifying the "herd mentality" that can overrun the stock market. Introducing Nikola Motors, Trevor Milton's 2014 dream that would transform the car business with electric and hydrogen-powered cars. Nikola didn't merely sell cars; it sold a vision for the future, and investors from all over the globe were ready to partake in this revolutionary adventure.

But a very different reality lay beneath the veneer of innovation and astronomically high valuations. The Nikola One truck, shown in a promotional video as an engineering marvel, was just coasting downhill, powered by gravity rather than revolutionary technology.

The shocking news served as a harsh wake-up call about the perils of investing in a herd mentality. Without solid evidence, even the most promising initiatives might be little more than mirages; the trust and investments of many, especially retail investors, were left to face the harsh reality as the truck went downhill.

In the haste to invest, we must not lose sight of reality; this incident serves as a lesson on the crucial requirement of due diligence, more than it does as a cautionary tale about a corporation.

These all attracted huge investor money.

CHAPTER 16

Emotional Investing

Picture yourself navigating the financial world when emotions, rather than rationality, are in charge. When investors let their emotions guide their investment decision, they may make hasty trades based on rumors rather than data. Scientific studies have shown that following this course of action usually results in more disappointment than satisfaction.

The real kicker, though, is that being a successful investor is about more than simply numbers; it's also about knowing and controlling your own thoughts.

The years 2020 and 2021 were marked by a pandemic of social boredom. Concerns about the public's mental health and wellness were caused by restrictions on travel, sports and other forms of physical exercise. New cars, toys, furniture, appliances, and pets were among the items purchased by irate consumers, all driven by stimulus checks and cheap or free loans from the government.

Because live sports betting was not an option, the smaller investor started focusing on the stock market instead. At the time, one of the main motivating factors was a lack of respect for conventional wisdom. While long-term investors like Warren Buffett exercised caution when the pandemic first broke out, unknown social media celebrities didn't.

The bias of seeking out or interpreting data in a manner that supports one's previous views or theories is called confirmation bias. When investors see stories or statistics that back up their investments or market opinions, they may ignore stories or data that show the opposite.

The overconfidence bias causes investors to take unnecessary risks in trading or predicting outcomes because they believe they are more capable than they actually are. There is a risk that investors will put too much faith in their own expertise, control, and ability to predict how the market will behave. Many take their confidence for expertise.

Too much weight given to the initial piece of data (the "anchor") seen when making a choice is known as anchoring bias. What this means for investors is that past performance may matter more than present or future fundamentals when deciding whether to buy a stock – a common trait amongst newbies and professionals alike.

The principle that individuals would rather not lose money than earn the same amount is known as loss aversion. As a result, investors may "lock in" gains by selling winning stocks too soon and holding losing stocks for too long in the hopes of breaking even.

Success is derived from two main places: rigorous conduct and astute analysis. Recognizing and overcoming one's own prejudices is just as important as knowing one's numbers. When investors let their preconceptions influence their decisions, the market becomes a psychological battleground. The key to success may lie in recognizing these biases and acting accordingly.

There is, however, a catch. Your inherent biases are a part of being human, just like everyone else's. Keeping cognitive mistakes at bay requires a delicate balancing act between being optimistic during booms and pessimistic during busts. Recognizing and controlling your biases along with combining analytical rigor and behavioral discipline will help you win more. It's about more than just outperforming the market; it's about outperforming yourself.

Be Like Buffett

In our quest for quick wins in the stock market, we often overlook the wisdom of patience. Consider Warren Buffett, the embodiment of investing patience. He's not chasing the fast buck; he's searching for value – companies undervalued but rich in long-term potential. Steady profits, positive cash flow, minimal debt.

Simple, yet profound. His method? Diligence. He dives deep into a company's essence, beyond the numbers, to its core operations and leadership. The message? Slow down. Look closer. The secret to investment success lies not in the speed of your decisions but in their depth and understanding. Let's not be hasty investors but wise ones, learning from the maestro himself.

Conclusion

In the dance with the markets, embrace humility as your shield. The market, a cunning teacher, favors the humble and the curious. Each investment tells a story of risk and reward, demanding your keen insight. Ask yourself: Are you chasing trends or guided by knowledge? Let your research lead the way, arm yourself with understanding, not just hope. In this ever-changing game, remember, certainty is the greatest illusion.

As you move forward, recognize that the market's greatest trick is disguising risks as opportunities. Start with the risks; let wisdom light your path to informed decisions. In a world of illusions, your clarity is your most powerful tool.